THINKING ABOUT EDUCATION SERIES
FOURTH EDITION
Jonas F. Soltis, *Editor*

The revised and expanded Fourth Edition of this series builds on the strengths of the previous editions. Written in a clear and concise style, these books speak directly to preservice and in-service teachers. Each offers useful interpretive categories and thought-provoking insights into daily practice in schools. Numerous case studies provide a needed bridge between theory and practice. Basic philosophical perspectives on teaching, learning, curriculum, ethics, and the relation of school to society are made readily accessible to the reader.

PERSPECTIVES ON LEARNING
D. C. Phillips and Jonas F. Soltis

THE ETHICS OF TEACHING
Kenneth A. Strike and Jonas F. Soltis

CURRICULUM AND AIMS
Decker F. Walker and Jonas F. Soltis

SCHOOL AND SOCIETY
Walter Feinberg and Jonas F. Soltis

APPROACHES TO TEACHING
Gary D Fenstermacher and Jonas F. Soltis

FOURTH EDITION

SCHOOL
and SOCIETY

WALTER FEINBERG
University of Illinois at Urbana–Champaign

JONAS F. SOLTIS
Teachers College, Columbia University

Teachers College
Columbia University
New York and London

Published by Teachers College Press, 1234 Amsterdam Avenue, New York, NY 10027

Copyright © 2004 by Teachers College, Columbia University

All rights reserved. No part of this publication may be reproduced or transmitted in any form or by any means, electronic or mechanical, including photocopy, or any information storage and retrieval system, without permission from the publisher

Library of Congress Cataloging-in-Publication Data

Feinberg, Walter, 1937–
    School and society / Walter Feinberg, Jonas F. Soltis.—4th ed.
       p. cm. — (Thinking about education series)
    Includes bibliographical references.
    ISBN 0-8077-4496-4 (pbk. : alk. paper)
      1. Educational sociology. I. Soltis, Jonas F. II. Title. III. Series.
    LC191.F4 2004
    302.43′2—dc22   2004048008

ISBN 0-8077-4496-4 (paper)

Printed on acid-free paper

Manufactured in the United States of America

11   10   09   08   07   06   05   04   8   7   6   5   4   3   2   1

Contents

Acknowledgments   ix

PART I
THE RELATION OF SCHOOL TO SOCIETY   1

Chapter 1
WHAT THIS BOOK IS ABOUT   3
    Factory Prep   3
    An Imaginary Society   4
    Three Schools of Thought   6
    The Form of the Book   8

PART II
SCHOOLING AS SOCIALIZATION AND PROGRESS   13

Chapter 2
THE FUNCTIONALIST PERSPECTIVE ON SCHOOLING   15
    Functionalism   15
    Equality of Educational Opportunity   20
    Educational Reform: Three Cases   22
    Assimilation, Political Socialization, and Modernization   24

Chapter 3
FUNCTIONAL THEORY, POLICY, AND PROBLEMS   29
    Historical Impediments and Compensatory Education   30
    Intellectual and Cultural Impediments   31
    Poverty   35
    Problems with Functionalism   36

PART III
SCHOOLING AS LEGITIMATION AND
REPRODUCTION   41

Chapter 4
MARXIST THEORY AND EDUCATION   43
    Conflict Theory and Functionalism   43
    Marxist Theory   46
    Class Consciousness, False Consciousness,
        and Hegemony   49
    Marxism, Neo-Marxism, and Education   53
    A Neo-Marxist Interpretation of Schooling in
        Capitalist Society   56

Chapter 5
THE HIDDEN CURRICULUM REVISITED   59
    A Theory of Cultural Reproduction   62
    Student Subculture and the Working Class   65
    Puzzles, Problems, and Prospects   68
    Foucault and the Post Modern Move Beyond Marxism   70
    Feminism as a Form of Conflict Theory   74

PART IV
INTERPRETATION AND THE SOCIAL FUNCTION
OF SCHOOLING   79

Chapter 6
THE INTERPRETIVIST POINT OF VIEW   81
    An Argument for the Interpretivist Point of View   84
    The Active Quality of Mind   86
    The Role of Interpretation in Social Science   87
    Interpretive Scholarship in Education   93

Chapter 7
MEANING AND MESSAGES; SCHOOLING AND SOCIALIZATION   98
    Hermeneutics and Interpretation   102
    Interpretation and Socialization   104
    Interpretation, Socialization, and Legitimation   107
    Objections to the Interpretivist Approach   109
    What Is at Stake?   110

PART V
CASES AND DISPUTES   113

Chapter 8
CASES AND DISPUTES   115
    Student Government   117
    The Roots of School Failure   119
    The Hidden Curriculum   121
    National Reports on Education   122
    The Geography Lesson   123
    Resource Allocation   124
    College or Workforce?   126
    Individual Differences and Equal Opportunity   128
    Social Reproduction   129
    Equal but Separate   131
    Education for Work   132
    Workforce School   133
    Class Bias?   134
    Social Studies   136
    Interpretation and Ethical Relativism 136
    The New Student   137
    Mainstream or Not?   138
    Social Conditioning and Freedom   140
    Interpretation and Epistemic Relativism 141
    A Third-World School System   142
    The Curriculum   143

Notes   149

Annotated Bibliography   153

Acknowledgments

We wrote the first edition of this book in the early 1980s and then added some new ideas to the second and third editions in the 1990s. This fourth edition keeps much of the original material from the previous editions, which we feel is still relevant as a way to think about school and society today in the twenty-first century, and adds a new section on the impact of federal and state mandates regarding standards, accountability, and high-stakes testing on schools. We have also updated the bibliography with the able assistance of James Scott Johnston. Our cases remain a very strong part of the usefulness of this text, adding relevance and reality to the ideas we discuss. For their comments on the manuscript for the first edition, we thank Eric Bredo, Charles Harrington, Eleanor Feinberg, and Alan Peshkin. Also, Karl Hostetler served adeptly as its research assistant, and Frances Simon processed and reprocessed many of its pages. Nancy Soltis processed the additions for the second, third, and fourth editions. Comments from colleagues and students formed our judgments about the need to add sections on postmodernism and feminism to the third edition. Through all four editions, we were fortunate at Teachers College Press to have the editorial advice of Susan Liddicoat and the production supervision of Peter Sieger and Karl Nyberg.

Part I

THE RELATION
OF SCHOOL
TO SOCIETY

Chapter 1

What This Book Is About

This is a book about the relationship between school and society. In it we want to invite you to think about what schools do besides teach the three Rs and the other school subjects. As you will see, schools communicate implicit as well as explicit messages to their students. To begin, we will ask you to imagine yourself in a school that is probably quite different from the ones you have attended. It will be an imaginary school, but it is not an impossible kind of school to have in a society like ours, even though we do not think any like it really exist. As you read about it in the paragraphs that follow, ask yourself what else is being taught and learned at Factory Prep besides the school subjects. You might also pause and think about your own schooling. Did its organization and practices reflect how your own society works? What did you learn in school?

Factory Prep

Imagine a school where there is never any homework. Work is only done in school, because that is where the machines are. Students punch a time card when they arrive in each classroom. They work at their studies only until the bell rings and then punch out. At the end of each week, every student receives a paycheck. Each student has a computer terminal and works at his or her own pace. There is a meter on each terminal, and the teacher can read off how much the student has accomplished during the week. This allows the school to reward students in relation to their productivity.

Courses are chosen on an elective system. Of course, the study of some subjects pays more than the study of others. If there is a shortage of scientists, courses in science offer a very high rate of pay. Because math is "harder" than English literature and mastery of math requires more "skill" than mastery of history, each hour of school work in math pays twice that devoted to literature and one-and-one-half times that given to history.

At the end of the week, each student's time on various subjects is computed at the appropriate rate, and a check for the amount earned is issued. A portion of each high school student's pay is withheld and goes to the elementary school to be used to pay younger, inexperienced students at a cheaper rate for their work. The high school is funded by withholdings from students in postsecondary technical schools and colleges. These, in turn, are funded by business and industry, which promise jobs and commensurate pay to students who successfully complete a secondary or postsecondary education. The workers' withholdings in business and industry pay for postsecondary schools.

Student checks at Factory Prep are cashed only at the school shopping mall, where students buy records and clothes, go to movies and play arcade games, or just socialize between classes or after school. When the cost of such things goes up, students tend to choose more difficult courses and work harder to keep up. But eventually their accustomed standard of leisure living declines, and they band together and demand higher rates. Student representatives bargain with the principal and faculty and usually reach an agreement. When they do not, the students strike. Because the principal and teachers are paid by the Board of Education with a percentage of the profits from the school shopping mall (and nonworking students are buying less), they have less income. These economic pressures on both sides usually produce an acceptable agreement fairly quickly.

With a little imagination, we are sure you could go on describing aspects of Factory Prep. It should be clear that besides learning subjects, these students are learning how to be workers in a society that recognizes the legitimacy of organized labor. But they are also learning other things about consumption, leisure, money, civic responsibility, and more. No doubt you could identify other things learned in this imaginary case, as well as some things besides subjects that you learned in your own schooling. In the last chapter of this book, called "Cases and Disputes," we have provided a number of realistic cases of school practices and imaginary disputes for you to use to extend your thinking about issues and ideas raised in each chapter. Throughout the text, we will suggest relevant cases and disputes for your consideration. Here we suggest a case from chapter 8 called "Student Government," which deals with the learning of good citizenship. It presents a more realistic situation than our imaginary Factory Prep and raises some interesting issues about what is learned in school besides subjects.

An Imaginary Society

Let's try to view the relation between school and society from another perspective. Instead of the industrial, high-tech, Western society presupposed in the first example, imagine an agricultural society with common ownership of gardens and animals and the communal sharing of work and food. In this society there are no permanent or elected leaders and no paid public servants. Instead, on a rotating basis for one month each year, all adults serve as teachers in the school, judges in the court, council members, police, and in other such necessary social service capacities. Except for this public service, most adults spend their lives tending the gardens and the animals.

There is always time for celebration and festivals, however, and the people thoroughly enjoy this major diversion from their workaday world. Song, dance, and storytelling are the central activities at festival time, and while the colorful design of costumes is important, there is not much other effort at visual art in this society. Song seems to be the dominant art form of public expression, even in the work place. Weeders and planters go down the rows chanting and planting and pulling in unison. Almost every activity has a song to be sung with it. The storytelling at festival time is predominantly "historical"; that is, the stories tell of heroes and happenings in the life of the society. Standard stories are also told and retold in the daily lives of the people and serve as the bearers of their moral code and the justification of social practices. It is a peaceful society isolated from the outside world and without warring neighbors.

Even with such a brief sketch, it should be possible to imagine what schooling might be like in this society. You might want to pause for a few moments to think about it yourself before considering our guesses on the matter. What subjects might be taught? What kinds of things might the children be asked to do? What might a typical day or month look like in a school in this society?

We speculate that in this society's schools, students might take turns once a month being a class leader responsible for such things as feeding the fish, leading the morning rituals, delivering messages, and tidying up the room. They would probably be encouraged to help each other with their lessons and to work together in the classroom. Each day, class might begin with a song and with a fable and a discussion of its "moral." The history of the group, not the history of the world, would probably be a core subject, along with some version of the "theory and principles of agriculture." Years ago, when it was an even simpler society than it is today, the traditional songs and dances of the festivals would have been taught at home; now these songs and dances, along with storytelling, are taught in school. There would probably be no lessons in the visual arts. The children would work each day in the school garden and learn the appropriate songs for each gardening activity.

We could go on, but the point should be clear. We expect schools and societies to reflect each other, not just in terms of the subjects taught, but also with respect to how the school is organized and functions. These two examples show that, in different situations, society is reflected in different ways and to different degrees. Industrialized nations do not have schools like Factory Prep, but clearly their schools do reflect some aspects of an industrialized society—such as mass production, bureaucratic organization, unionization, and impersonalized, hierarchial decision making.

Three Schools of Thought

This book is about the ways in which we try to explain and understand the relationship between school and society. In the contemporary world, there are a number of competing kinds of explanations with a number of different labels. For convenience, we have chosen to group these explanations under the three umbrella terms *functionalism, conflict theory,* and *the interpretivist approach.* These are complex and sometimes overlapping schools of thought that we will explore more fully in the chapters that follow. To help you get a feeling for the idea that similar events can be explained in different ways, we will look back at the Factory Prep example, first through the eyes of an imaginary functionalist and then through the eyes of an imaginary conflict theorist.

The *functionalist* generally sees schools as serving to socialize students to adapt to the economic, political, and social institutions of that society. In the Factory Prep case, students were learning how to be workers, consumers, taxpayers, and union members. They were also learning the traditional school subjects, of course. Learning these subjects is often called the "manifest function" of schools by functionalists. The manifest function refers to the clear and obvious intellectual purpose of schooling in society. However, the functionalist also sees schools serving a "latent" or not so visible function of producing people who share the basic economic, political, and cultural practices and norms of the society. Moreover, the functionalist sees the school as an integral, functioning part of society, vital to its continuation and survival. To convey this basic idea, functionalists often suggest that we view social institutions as analogous to parts of the body. Each functions to serve the needs and purposes of the whole. Thus a functionalist would see Factory Prep serving one of the most important institutional tasks in any society, socialization. For the functionalist, socialization means the effective molding of individuals to fit existing social practices and requirements.

A *conflict theorist* would generally view schooling as a social practice supported and utilized by those in power to maintain their dominance in the social order. In the social world of Factory Prep, there are clearly workers on the one hand and bosses and owners of businesses and industries on the other. Students in Factory Prep are learning to be workers, not bosses. They are also learning to be consumers, who are necessary for the maintenance of the "boss" class. Without the excessive consumption of nonnecessities, extensive profits could not be realized by the owners of big business and consumer industries. Financing the schools out of taxes on wages, rather than out of profits, may give workers the sense that they are supporting their schools; but what it really does, the conflict theorist would argue, is keep profits intact while forcing workers to pay for their own training. It should be clear that the conflict with which the conflict theorist is concerned is between classes, between the rich and poor, the workers and the capitalists, the powerful and the powerless. Many conflict theorists are Marxists, and in our treatment of conflict theory, we concentrate on its Marxist form. Marxists see social institutions functioning to preserve inequitable class relations in society, and they urge us to do something about it.

Obviously, functionalism and conflict theory are two very different ways of looking at the same social world and at the relation of school to society. One sees the school as an "organ" of society, like a heart or a lung, functioning properly to keep the "body politic" going. The other sees the school as an instrument of class domination serving to reproduce the workforce and maintain class relationships. Each offers different ways to explain what social forces are operating in the school.

A third way to look at the social world and the school we have called the interpretivist approach. It is better illustrated by our imaginary agricultural society, but it can be applied to the Factory Prep example as well. The *interpretivist* sees the social world as a world made up of purposeful actors who acquire, share, and interpret a set of meanings, rules, and norms that make social interaction possible. The social forces at work are shared meanings and interpreting individuals who interact in particular social contexts. In the school of the agricultural society, the children were acquiring a sense of their society's way of life by learning its traditional songs, its fables, its history, and its norms of cooperation and public service. They were also learning how to do things in that social setting. To understand and explain why a particular student or teacher did a particular thing in such a school, interpretivists would argue that we need to understand the way of life in that society and the ways of doing things in that school. They would also remind us that we need to learn the purposes of the individual actors and the social meanings that they share with others. How individuals interpret and understand their social situations is a central concern of the interpretivist.

Frequently interpretivists will use the analogy of a game to explain their view of the social world of meanings, rules, and purposes. One cannot play a game or engage in certain social activities without understanding what they are about and what is expected or allowed. Thus an interpretivist might look at Factory Prep and say the students have learned the rules of the "game of school," which include, among other things, how to increase or decrease their income from classroom work, how to satisfy their desire for leisure time, and what is allowed in terms of confrontation with the administration. They then decide whether it is worth the extra effort to increase their income by taking hard classes. They also decide which things to spend their money on, and, in case of a grievance, they decide whether to go on strike. They do these things as individuals with some degree of freedom, but always within the constraints of their shared understanding of the "game of school" and their willingness to play it. Some drop out, of course, refusing to play the game.

Clearly there is some overlap in our general descriptions of these three approaches to explaining the relation of school to society. This is not only because they deal with the same phenomenon of people learning to be members of a social group, but also because in reality our three categories contain much similarity as well as much variation. In the world of contemporary research and scholarship, there are functionalists who recognize conflict and deal with it functionally; there are conflict theorists who are not Marxists; and there are interpretivists who are very difficult, if not impossible, to distinguish from either conflict theorists or functionalists. Even so, we think that for the novice the three-approach scheme of this book will do more good than harm in providing a framework in which to see how modern scholars and researchers have been thinking about the relation of school to society. We merely caution you at the outset not to take these labels too strictly. They are heuristic devices. The point of this book is to help you think about school and society by seeing how others have thought about it, not by learning how to apply one label or another to the thinkers or to school situations.

The Form of the Book

Part II will treat functionalism in depth, showing its strengths and some of its limitations. Functionalism is the dominant form of sociological explanation in our industrial-technical-scientific society. It claims for itself the status of scientific explanation. In Part III we will seek the roots of conflict theory in Marx and examine contemporary Marxist studies of schooling as the legitimation of class inequities. In Part IV we will explore interpretivist theory and qualitative research as they illuminate the relation of schooling to society and help us to see some points of similarity between the functionalist and conflict theorists' approaches.

In each part we have included summaries of a few empirical studies that have been inspired by the approach under discussion. Our objective is to show you how each approach provides a different way for trying to understand specific school practices. It is our hope that you will not simply learn the names of researchers and their approaches to the understanding of the relation between school and society. We are mainly concerned with helping you to think about that relation for yourself and to develop your own understanding of it.

How can teachers make sense of conflicting explanations of the way schools are organized today, the public controversies over schooling, and various attempts by society to change the schools? We think they need some philosophical and social perspective, and that is what this book is about. Lest you think these theories are esoteric and nonapplicable to your everyday world, in Part V we have supplied a collection of realistic cases and disputes to stimulate your thinking and to raise ethical as well as intellectual issues. These cases and debates will illustrate the relation of theory to practice in a way that may be new to you. The theories dealt with in this book will not tell you what to do; they will help you to think seriously about what you and other educators are doing. They also will give you some perspective on current school- and society-related controversies.

Controversy over the social purpose of teaching and schooling is not new, and our schools have often been criticized from various quarters. In the early part of the twentieth century, for example, major debates took place regarding the proper role of the school in "Americanizing" the immigrants who were entering the country from Europe. At mid-century, the public schools were severely criticized for failing to prepare a sufficient number of people who would be able to take up advanced training in science and engineering. Less than a decade later, the schools came under attack as being too much concerned with subject matter and too little concerned with the growth of the individual child. They were criticized for their "rigid," "sterile" curriculum and for failing to serve adequately the cause of equal opportunity. Over the span of writing four editions of this book, we have seen recurrent forms of these issues. The contemporary concern over multicultural curricula reflects some of the issues developed earlier regarding the appropriate education for immigrants, and it also reflects the concern for using the schools to provide economically disadvantaged groups and ethnic minorities with greater opportunities. At the same time, there is increased concern that schools are failing to teach the "basic skills" involved in reading, writing, and calculation. American schools are being criticized for not producing a sufficiently educated workforce that will allow us to compete successfully with other nations in our global economy. Moreover, declining scores on standardized tests and increasing school violence, drug use, teenage pregnancy, and dropout rates have been taken as signs that the schools are failing to provide the structure and discipline that many people believe education and society require. At the same time, we are witnessing contemporary controversies in the educational research community over how best to do research that will speak to these problems and help teachers and schools to be more effective. The earlier, almost single-minded reliance on objective quantitative research is being supplemented by an increasing body of qualitative research on the subjective and local dimensions of schooling.

Whatever the particular controversy in education may be, it is often the case that insufficient attention is paid to the social context in which the issues take on importance. There is a strong tendency to overlook social, political, and cultural factors that have helped to create the situation—and that also serve to create both possibilities for and limitations on what schools and teachers can do at any particular time. Without such a perspective, teachers, who have been struggling to meet previously defined needs, are often blamed for inadequately addressing a newly defined one. For students training to be teachers, the problems can be especially acute. For example, students trained during a time when academic rigor was stressed may find the emphasis shifting to concerns for greater flexibility, equality, or individual differences as they undertake their teaching careers. Without an understanding of some of the factors that generate these shifts and without the tools to appraise them, frustration, disenchantment, and alienation are likely to result. While it is unlikely that any single person, no matter how experienced, can predict with great accuracy the shifting perceptions of social need and the future demands that will be made on the school, it is possible to bring the social context of education back into focus if you know what to look for and have a framework for doing so. Part of what we attempt to do in this book is to help you develop such a framework and obtain some practice in using it to think about the problems of schools. This will require your willingness to reflect upon and critically examine your own ideas about the role of school in society.

Schools are a human invention. They have a history. They change forms either in reaction to social forces or because of our conscious attempt to change them. Thus, participants in the schools and in society give schooling a structure; but schools also structure those who work in them and pass through them. We cannot offer a history of the school as a social institution here. However, it is important for you to keep a historical perspective in mind. It is important to recognize that schools were not always structured the way they are today. The future structure of education may depend upon educators who, we hope, have become fully aware of both the positive and negative aspects of the current structure of schools. This in turn should give professional educators a sense of their potential to shape schooling in positive ways.

To give you an overview of the three positions we will treat in the book, we have provided in chapter 8 an imaginary debate between their proponents that you might want to read and think about before going on. It deals with their different kinds of explanations of "The Roots of School Failure."

Part II

SCHOOLING
AS SOCIALIZATION
AND PROGRESS

Chapter 2

The Functionalist Perspective on Schooling

Functionalism

Functionalism is a general theoretical orientation about how social events and institutions are to be viewed. It is an orientation that has been especially prominent in the fields of anthropology (the study of culture) and sociology (the study of society). Its basic insight, however, is drawn from the field of biology. Functionalists note that the various systems of a biological organism serve different survival functions. In mammals, for example, the stomach, small intestine, and other organs digest food, while the heart pumps blood, thereby bringing oxygen from the lungs to different parts of the body. There are other organs that remove waste and still others that function in the reproduction process. Other species, such as fish, may have organs that are structured quite differently but serve the same survival needs. Carrying this insight from the biological to the social sphere, functionalists argue that if we want to understand a certain social practice or institution, we must consider the way in which it serves to further the survival of the social system as a whole. For example, if we want to understand the role that mass, compulsory schooling serves in contemporary society, we would be advised to explore the social needs it serves and the ways it works to meet those needs. For the functionalist, there is a similar kind of explanation for such seemingly different questions as why certain animal species kill some of their newborn, why different species of fireflies display different coded lights, why physicians have high incomes, and why schools use standardized tests. The point is that each question is answered in terms of some basic survival need that is being served.

Just as the different parts and behaviors of an organism can be understood in terms of the function they serve in meeting the needs of survival, so, too, the functionalist argues, can the practices and the institutions of a society be explained in terms of meeting certain social survival needs. Because different environments require different responses, the way in which such needs are met may differ. However, an adequate understanding of a social institution or a practice must be grounded in an understanding of the need that it functions to serve and the way that it does so. Thus, functionalists tend to look at social institutions and practices in terms of their contribution to the adaptation and adjustment of the total social system.[1]

Consider the selection, training, and rewarding of physicians and teachers in our society. From a functionalist point of view we would seem to need both to survive, but how might we explain the large differences in income, status, and prestige that exist between doctors and teachers? A functionalist explanation would go something like this: There are many tasks in a society that a large number of people can perform, and so a large wage is not required to encourage people to undertake these tasks. However, there are some needs in modern society that can be served only by the special talents of a relatively few people. The practice of medicine is one of these, and the development of this talent requires many years of training and education. Therefore, as encouragement for talented people to undertake this special sacrifice, society provides extra incentives. Higher income and enhanced status are society's ways of providing such incentives and of insuring that these specialized needs are met. As long as many more people have the talent to become teachers than to become doctors, then the difference in status and income will remain.

In a similar way, functionalists argue that all societies require that their members perform different tasks. Selection, socialization, and training processes are needed to assure that jobs, even unpleasant or demanding ones, get done. Even in primitive societies, role differentiation will be found as some members hunt, others gather, and still others prepare food. In primitive societies, however, role differentiation is not intense, and one member's contribution to the society can often be seen by all other members. Because contributions made by different people performing different roles are visible to all and everyone participates in the tribal rituals, the group develops a shared value system and cognitive orientation; thus their sense of group solidarity is maintained.

For the functionalists, *role differentiation* and *social solidarity* are the two primary requirements of social life. They must be present in primitive and modern societies alike. In primitive societies these requirements can be met through the informal education that occurs within the family and the community. In highly complex, modern societies, however, where roles change from one generation to the next, a more formal structure is required to assure that the education of the young takes place and that role differentiation and group solidarity are achieved. A system of universal, compulsory, public education is established to accomplish this.

Compulsory education is also able to assure that older, dysfunctional habits, attitudes, and loyalties are replaced by newer, more functional ones. Compulsory education facilitates the development of new skills that the continuous expansion of technology requires. Just think, for example, of the changes being wrought in our society and our schools today by the advent of computers.

From the functionalist point of view, universal compulsory education is closely related to the requirements of industrial society. Schools perform in a formal way those basic tasks that simpler societies are able to perform informally through the ongoing activity of the family, the community, or the tribe. For example, in most traditional societies, children learn to work by watching their parents and other adults working and by participating in that work at increasing levels of responsibility. In modern societies, children have little opportunity to watch their parents work, and schools must now teach many of the requisite skills and attitudes.

This brings us to another feature that is often associated with functionalism. This feature is a stage theory that is used to explain the "development" from simple, traditional social structures to more complex, modern ones. Functionalists who accept a stage theory believe that the movement from traditional to modern society can be explained in terms of different kinds of functional integration. Wilbert Moore, in his summary of functionalism, describes one widely accepted model as follows:

> Stage one is the functionally integrated and therefore relatively static traditional society; stage two comprises the transitional process of structural alteration in the direction of modernity; stage three is the functionally integrated fully . . . modernized society.[2]

This extension of functionalism has sparked considerable debate both inside and outside of the functionalist camp. Some argue that a stage theory is too ambitious. There is not just one pattern of development that holds for all societies, nor possibly should all societies become "modernized." Others note that the image presented of modern society as essentially democratic and free justifies morally questionable attempts to change the nature of traditional societies. Nevertheless, while stage theory has not been fully accepted by all functionalists, it has been an important feature of the work of some of its major advocates.[3] Moreover, it has had significant influence on matters of educational policy in Third World countries.

Those who accept a stage theory of development are often quite explicit in proclaiming the benefits of modern societies over traditional ones. In their view modern societies are able to satisfy more needs for more people, and compulsory schooling is seen as an essential part of this process. School provides the role differentiation and solidarity that in most traditional societies are developed through other means. In traditional societies individuals have little chance to advance beyond the station into which they were born. Training for positions of leadership is only available to those with the appropriate birthright. In contemporary industrial society schools replace parental status as the principal selection mechanism. Moreover, they provide the training appropriate for participation in the social order at a certain level. Many functionalists argue that modern schools perform these tasks in a much more efficient, fair, and humane way than they have been performed in societies without a system of universal, compulsory education.

Many functionalists believe that schools are the essential transformation mechanism between life in the family and life as an adult in a modern, urban, industrial society. One of the most succinct descriptions of this functionalist view of schooling is provided by Robert Dreeben in *On What Is Learned in School.*[4] Dreeben argues that schoolchildren learn to function according to the norms that are appropriate to economic and political life in the modern world. Norms are standards used to govern one's conduct in appropriate situations. Dreeben observes that such learning not only derives from the subject matter that is explicitly taught in the school but also happens as children begin to function according to the organizational patterns that are a fundamental part of school life. In this latter case, it is the *ways* things are taught, rather than *what* is taught, that enable such norms to be learned. According to Dreeben, four key norms are learned in school as a youngster passes from the lower to the higher grades and from membership in the family to membership in the society. He calls these norms "independence," "achievement," "universalism," and "specificity."[5] He believes that these norms are essential to being an effectively functioning member of a modern, industrial, democratic society. He also believes that they can only be taught effectively and on a large scale in schools.

The norm of *independence* refers to the learning that occurs when children come to take responsibility for their own action and to acknowledge that others have a right to hold them accountable for such action. Schoolchildren learn this norm through such things as sanctions against cheating and plagiarism. These sanctions prepare students for adult life and for the kind of occupations that will require them to take on individual responsibility. The adoption of this norm teaches children to be personally accountable for their own performance. Learning the norm of *achievement* is learning that one will be judged by one's performance and not, for example, by one's effort or good intentions. Students also learn to judge their own performance against that of others. Here some students must learn to cope with failure and to acknowledge the greater skills of others in certain areas of performance.

The norms of *universalism* and *specificity* refer to the treatment of a person in terms of some standardized basis of comparison. For example, for certain purposes, all first graders (specificity) are considered appropriate to compare with one another (a universal group). These norms are reflected in the schools in many different ways. For example, when a child's request for an excuse for a late assignment is met with the response, "If I make an exception for you, I will have to make one for everyone else," the norm of universalism is being expressed. If the teacher says, "John is a member of the basketball team and so is excused from tonight's assignment because of the game," the norm of specificity is being invoked.

Universalism, according to Dreeben, refers to the uniform treatment of individuals as members of one or more specific categories, for example, team members, bus students, or graduating seniors. The important point about learning to accept the norm of universalism is that, in doing so, one becomes willing in certain circumstances to put aside one's individuality and be treated as a member of a group. Universalism requires the same treatment for all. For instance, all team members may be required to attend all practice sessions. *Specificity* allows for exceptions to be made. The coach may excuse a team member from practice because the player observes a religious holiday not observed by others on the team. *Particularism* makes illegitimate exceptions. If the coach gives special advantage to one youngster because he happens to be the child of a fellow teacher, we have an instance of particularism. The norm of specificity is related to that of universalism. It speaks to our obligation to treat people similarly only on the basis of the specific categories that are relevant to the task at hand. Students learn that exceptions can be made only if they are made on legitimate grounds. For some activities the number of relevant categories for specificity may be quite large. For example, the elementary school teacher may find age, ability, maturity, and family stability to be relevant. The high school teacher may only consider performance in one subject to be relevant.

The four norms may or may not be taught in the family as well as in the school. When such norms are taught in the family, however, there is a difference. Unlike the family, Dreeben observes, the school provides youngsters with a group of peers against whose performances their own individual performance can be judged. In school youngsters are grouped together according to age, and this provides them with a visible point against which to compare their own independence and achievement. Comparison with others as peers is also basic to learning the norms of universalism and specificity, and many such opportunities present themselves in school.

As a functionalist, Dreeben believes that the four norms of independence, achievement, universalism, and specificity are precisely those that are required to act as a worker and a citizen in contemporary industrial society. By learning to accept the four norms that are transmitted through participation in school life, students develop the "psychological capacities that enable them to participate in the major institutional areas of society, to occupy the component social positions of these areas, and to cope with the demands and exploit the opportunities that these positions characteristically present."[6]

Equality of Educational Opportunity

You can see the influence of these norms, which you may have learned in school, by observing your own reaction to the following fictional advertisement: "Wanted, white Christian male, Ivy League graduate, for managerial work in a major marketing firm. Excellent opportunities for advancement."

There was a time when advertisements similar to this were not unusual, and many ethnic groups have stories about such overt discrimination. Today such an advertisement would clearly demand attention. It violates many people's sense of fairness (as well as the laws against discrimination) because it stipulates qualifications that seem to be irrelevant for successful performance in the position. Dreeben and other functionalists believe that the unfavorable reaction that would likely greet an advertisement of this kind can be attributed to the role that schools have played in developing the psychological attitudes that a commitment to the norms of universalism and achievement entails. We have become used to expecting that rewards will be granted on the basis of achievement and merit. Thus, the norms developed in school are related to an important ethical principle that is associated with contemporary industrial societies—the principle of equal opportunity.

The idea of equal opportunity means that individuals are to be chosen for certain roles and rewarded on the basis of *achieved*, rather than *ascribed*, characteristics. An ascribed characteristic is one that belongs to a person by virtue of his or her birth and background. Wherever political office, income, or rights are determined on the basis of family background alone, then we have a situation in which rewards are distributed according to ascribed qualities. When factors that are irrelevant to the task at hand are discounted, and a person is rewarded according to performance or to qualities that signal a promise for high-level performance, then we have a situation in which rewards are distributed according to achieved qualities. In most instances people will identify social-class background, race, religion, and sex as irrelevant, ascribed characteristics, and they will identify talent, ability, and motivation as relevant, achieved ones.

Functionalists give three reasons for the movement from ascribed to achieved rewards in modern societies. First, it is thought that the ever-expanding skills required by industrial society often render obsolete the skills passed on by the family or the local community. Thus, to reward qualities that have been passed on from one generation to the next may well be to retard the development of the new knowledge and skills required to meet modern needs. Second, the expanding need for new skills requires that opportunities be opened to talented people from groups that have traditionally been denied them. Third, political stability requires that those who have not been rewarded, as well as those who have, believe that they competed under a fair system of rules. Thus, the ideal of equal opportunity is thought to be not only ethically sound but also consistent with the requirements of stability in modern society.

It should be recalled that the transition from the personal life of the family to modern bureaucratic life described by the functionalists does not necessarily take place on the conscious level. If we ask teachers what they are doing at any particular moment, they are likely to answer in very specific ways, with such typical responses as "I am teaching spelling" or "I am working with the children on fractions." Seldom will teachers respond with comments like "I am teaching my students to judge themselves and others according to relevant categories" or "I am teaching them how to function in bureaucracies." Yet, according to the functionalists, this is precisely what is being accomplished. The interesting question to ask and answer is "How?"

The idea of the "hidden curriculum" has been one of the concepts that has been used to explain the school's role in making possible the transition from life in the family to a life of work and citizenship. The hidden curriculum refers to the organizational features and routines of school life that provide the structure needed to develop the psychological dispositions appropriate for work and citizenship in industrial society. The waiting in line, the vying for the teacher's attention, the sanctions against "cheating," the scheduling of activities according to the demands of the clock, all contribute to the development of behavior required by modern institutions. The student learns to channel and control impulses according to the institutionally approved patterns of behavior.[7]

Educational Reform: Three Cases

Functionalism has served as more than just a scientific theory used to understand the role that schools and other institutions play in society. It has also served as a theoretical guide for people interested in the reform and improvement of modern society. In other words, it has served as both the scientific foundation and the justification for many different kinds of educational reform. The use of functionalism by educational reformers is quite understandable. Once it is recognized that modern schooling is required to meet the needs of contemporary society, then it is quite a natural step to try to identify the precise nature of those needs and to mold educational policy to try to meet them more effectively. Much of educational reform has been built on the functionalist view that schools serve to help people adapt to the changing life of modern society. When adaptation becomes a problem and dysfunction results, it is quite reasonable for some people to think of schooling as a way to correct it. We can illustrate the connection between functionalism and educational reform by considering some imaginary cases.

First, imagine that you are not only a functionalist but also the head of state of a nation that just gained independence from a colonial power. The state you govern contains two tribes that are relatively equal in size and power. However, these major tribal groups have had a history of antagonism toward one another, and it was only resistance to the external colonial power that brought them together as a unified force. As leader of the new country, you are aware that within twenty years the northern tribal group will suffer a drought because the neighboring country is damming and diverting the river that flows first through its territory. You also know that only the food resources of the southern tribe will enable the north to avoid catastrophe. If the catastrophe is avoided, the northern tribal province should flourish and contribute much to the wealth of the entire nation. The difficulty that must be faced, however, is that present tribal loyalties would never allow the needed transfer of resources to take place. Without this transfer, the catastrophe cannot be avoided. Given this situation, it is decided that the only hope is to begin to shift personal loyalty from the tribal group to the nation. In order to do this, you begin to develop a public system of education and to offer special incentives for attendance. You mandate that the curriculum of the school will stress national purposes rather than tribal ones, and the most successful students will be offered the opportunity to attend the national, multitribal university and to take up leadership positions in the government. What else might you do?

Here is a second situation. Again imagine that you are a governmental leader in a society where the largest part of the population is in the agricultural sector. For the last three decades, however, there has been a decided movement toward urban areas. At the same time that factory production is becoming mechanized, so, too, is agricultural production. Because factory work is expanding rapidly, there is a need for more urban workers. On the farm, because of mechanization, fewer people are needed to produce more and more basic food products and fiber. However, as this urban migration is occurring, it is noticed that many of the basic work and sanitation habits that were appropriate for the farm are continuing in the city, even though they are no longer functional. For many of the new city dwellers, for example, money management is a problem. On the farm, basic needs could be more or less met without depending upon a long train of suppliers. In the city, this is not the case. There it is necessary to have the cash required to buy essential goods, and this means that the newcomer has to find a way both to make a wage and to manage it once it is made. In addition, the entire family structure is changing, and machines are reducing the need for child labor. Nevertheless, many children still work in factories. For those who do not, there are no relatives available to provide the attention and care they require while their parents work in factories. Many people have begun to feel that, without proper guidance, life in the city is becoming unhealthy for many children and that some new structure is needed for them. Yet as long as child labor is available, it provides a source of cheap workers for many businesses. Not to hire children is to operate at a competitive disadvantage. Schools are available, but many children do not attend them for a variety of reasons. The solution that you propose is to make school attendance compulsory into adolescence and to prohibit child labor. In this way no single business will be placed at an unfair advantage, and a substitute institution will take the place of the dwindling extended family. What other educational reforms might you propose to deal with the social problems that now exist in this society?

Imagine a third situation: A compulsory system of education has been operating in your country for a number of years, a reasonably high rate of literacy has been achieved, and for most groups the transition from rural to urban life has been accomplished. However, new technological advances have been developing that will require more scientists, engineers, and managers than are being produced by the present system. Over the years universities have remained the domain of the well-to-do, providing the children of this group with the polish needed to maintain their family position. However, if the new needs are not met, foreign competition threatens to overtake your nation's external markets and even to penetrate the home market. Your educational advisers have assured you that ample talent to fill the required need can be found among the general population. Unfortunately, few means exist to identify such talent, and the resources of higher education are not sufficient to train it. You respond by calling a meeting of leading educators, in which it is resolved to develop a fair national system of testing that will be used to identify talented members from all classes in the society who will be able to benefit from a university education. In addition, university educators promise to reform their curriculum by placing a new emphasis on science, mathematics, engineering, and business and by introducing graduate research programs that will assure a steady growth of knowledge in these areas. You agree to fund these proposals.

The three situations presented above are hypothetical; they do not attempt to describe the experience of any single country. They do, however, represent a functionalist approach to thinking about the establishment, maintenance, and change of a national system of compulsory education. In the situations above, at least three functions are represented. In the first instance, the school system will serve to establish a single, national identity and will thereby be used to overcome the strife created by conflicting tribal loyalties. In other words, it is serving the function of social integration. In the second instance, schooling is made compulsory in order to develop new habits and attitudes that changing times require. Here it is serving what may be called the function of social re-integration. In the third situation, the educational system will be fine tuned, or rationalized, to provide the higher-level skills demanded by international competition. In other words, it will be used to identify talent from all segments of society and to provide the training that higher-level skills demand. In this case, the school is serving the function of role differentiation. Before going on, you might want to consider the dispute over "National Reports on Education" in chapter 8.

Assimilation, Political Socialization, and Modernization

Many reformers, arguing along functionalist lines, view the school as society's primary instrument for meeting the demands of our modern political, social, and economic life. Specifically, they argue that schools must teach students to act according to democratic principles, to tolerate diversity, and to work in a specialized, highly technical economy. Add to these three political, social, and economic goals that a person should expect to be rewarded according to merit, and you have the basic elements required for developing and maintaining a modern, functional, meritocratic society. Three basic processes are related to this perception of the social function of the school. These are the school's role in cultural assimilation, political socialization, and modernization. The first two processes, assimilation and political socialization, are closely aligned to the functionalists' views on social integration and solidarity; the third process, modernization, is aligned to their views on role differentiation and development theory.

Assimilation is a cultural concept. It refers to the process whereby one group, usually a subordinate one, becomes indistinguishable from another group, usually a dominant one. As one group takes on the dress, speech patterns, tastes, attitudes, and economic status of the dominant group, the process of assimilation occurs. *Political socialization* is primarily a political concept. It is also, secondarily, a psychological one. In the context of modern society it refers to the widening of a person's political loyalty beyond the local group to the nation as a whole. It also refers to the process whereby a person comes to accept the decision-making process of modern democratic forms of government. *Modernization* is both an economic and a social concept. It refers to the development of the meritocratic, bureaucratic, and individualistic form of life that is associated with modern society and is viewed as a prerequisite for technological and economic development.

These three processes overlap. For example, assimilation involves, among other things, a change in the wants of the members of the newer groups. Modernization presupposes just such a change. After all, a meritocracy depends upon people wanting what it offers as rewards. Similarly, political socialization may be seen as a more specific case of assimilation. Nevertheless, while these processes overlap, they can be treated separately. In this section we examine the relationship between educational reform and the twin processes of assimilation and political socialization first and then look at educational reform and modernization.

As immigration from non-English-speaking areas increased in the early part of the twentieth century, reformers in the United States looked to the schools as a major instrument for assimilating new groups into what was called "the American way of life." People differed about the form that assimilation should take, however. Some believed that immigration should be restricted to those groups from Northern and Western Europe whose values were felt to be already in accord with the ideas of American culture. Others believed that immigration could be opened to groups from other countries if the schools proved able to "wash out" native cultural patterns and impose standards on the newcomers that were in keeping with "the American way of life." Still other reformers argued that each new culture had its own unique contribution to make to American society and that cultural identity should be nurtured in the schools. These people argued that the schools' responsibility should be to develop in each student a commitment to the ideal of a pluralistic society. Even though there were such different opinions about the form that social integration should take, there was agreement that political and technological concerns required a new pattern of assimilation.

Many educational reformers have looked to the schools to help assimilate new groups into the ongoing culture and to develop a common allegiance to democratic principles. There continue to be many differences among educators, as well as among political figures and within the general public, as to the best way to carry out this task. Some believe that schools should carry on a direct assault against political doctrines that are seen as alien to the values they associate with American democracy. Thus, during the Cold War some states passed laws mandating that schools teach courses about "the evils of communism." Others have argued that the schools should reflect in their own structures and curricula the decision-making process they associate with democratic forms of life. The encouragement of student government has been one response to this view. Others have proposed that students should be able to participate more fully in the planning and development of their own educational programs. Despite these differences, there has been agreement among many, both within education and outside it, that schools have an important role to play in the political socialization of the young.

Political socialization has a special importance in schooling in larger industrial societies, where much of the information that goes into the making of a political decision is not available to the public. When a government decides to raise taxes, go to war, or integrate a school, for instance, it requires a general acceptance by its citizenry of a number of things. First, it requires that the public believes that the government is acting as a representative of the general population. Second, it requires that the public believes that the government is acting in good faith. And third, it requires that each individual believes that the government has the support and the power to enforce its will. The first of these requirements means that students who will become citizens must develop faith in the process through which political representatives are chosen and their laws are made. The second requires that they have at least minimal faith in government officials and agencies. The third requires that students believe that most of the other people in the society have the kind of faith mentioned in the first two points above and therefore are in fact willing to act upon their government's orders. "The Geography Lesson" in chapter 8 raises issues about the relevance of politics to the classroom and what constitutes enlightened citizenship.

The role of the school in modernization is closely tied to both the cultural and the political functions of schooling. It refers to the development of a bureaucratic, individualized form of life in which the production (and to some extent the consumption) process is rationalized to meet the requirements of efficiency. When the term *modernization* is used by contemporary scholars and reformers, it is usually meant to indicate the process whereby a preindustrial society develops its agriculture, industry, and technology in a way that parallels the development that took place in Western Europe and the United States during and after the Industrial Revolution. Modernization theorists believe that economic growth in both agriculture and manufacturing depends upon the development of a market economy with a certain degree of centralized planning, the introduction of a meritocratic reward structure, and the development of a national bureaucracy.

Modernization theory has also emphasized the importance of the development of "human capital." This emphasis is of special significance to educators. The idea is that if the movement toward industrialization is to be effective, then there must be not only investment in machinery and capital equipment, there must also be a similar investment in the development of human skills. In other words, education has an *economic* value for the society at large, and a large part of the process of modernization involves identifying and training new talent so that it is able to make effective use of innovative technologies.[8]

The development of human capital is perceived as important in both technologically developed societies and in technologically developing ones. In developed societies it is perceived as a way to maintain the social wealth that past generations have established, while accelerating economic growth by bringing talented members from minority populations into the production process. Indeed, in some instances human capital theorists have argued that the greatest value may be reaped by investing more educational resources in groups that have previously been left behind in the educational process. In some circumstances the value added to the total wealth of a society may be increased more by investing additional resources in the education of an underachieving minority than in the already well-educated majority. In these circumstances human capital theory has provided strong arguments for opening educational opportunities to underrepresented minorities.

For technologically developing countries, the development of human capital is seen as essential in meeting the various "manpower" needs of the society at different occupational levels. Depending on the circumstances, there are a number of different kinds of choices that might be rational. For example, given a limited amount of resources, "manpower" planners might decide to allocate training funds for only a few positions requiring university-level education and concentrate the largest amount of educational resources for developing primary school education on a wider scale. In some situations it might be most cost-effective to train the nation's professional and technical elite in university facilities outside of the country, while using most of the educational resources within the country to build primary and secondary schools. Whatever the specific arrangement may be, the basic idea here is that the development of the educational system should be guided by and be functionally related to the overall requirements of the workforce.

In this chapter, we have described a functionalist approach to understanding and dealing with the relation of school to society. Functionalists view society as analogous to a biological organism whose various parts have evolved in an integrated way to meet needs and enhance the capacity for survival. From this analogy, the functionalist argues that schools serve to meet some of the essential needs of modern society. There is an important difference between social and biological functionalism, however. Organisms cannot readily change their organs nor alter their imprinted behaviors. Societies and schools can and do change, sometimes rapidly and radically. Some changes are brought about by the force of events, but others are consciously intended. Functionalism offers a way of thinking about the structuring, organizing, and reforming of schools in order to serve the perceived needs and purposes of society. But when this is done, some people get uncomfortable with the idea of manipulating people to achieve social ends. Before we go on to introduce the conflict theorists, who see schooling as a form of control by the classes in power, we will review in the next chapter some of the criticisms and problems to be found within functionalism. At this point, however, you might want to consider "Resource Allocation" in chapter 8, a case that brings into sharper focus ideas dealt with in this chapter and raises difficult questions about social needs and social justice.

Chapter 3

Functional Theory, Policy, and Problems

The principle of equal opportunity plays an important role in functionalist theory. The rewarding of talent is viewed as a necessary condition of modernization. Thus, this principle has become a most important guide for educational reform. In the ideal, functionally organized, modern society, individuals with equal talent and motivation to perform in an area of comparable need would be rewarded equally.

Many reformers have come to believe that this principle cannot be effectively brought into play without the institutionalization of a prior and related principle—the ideal of equality of *educational* opportunity. Whereas the principle of equality of opportunity directs that people should be rewarded according to their talents and not according to accidental factors such as family, race, sex, or religion, the principle of equal educational opportunity directs that individuals should have an equal chance to develop their talents. Educational reformers have argued that the schools should be the principal means for providing equal educational opportunity.

Given this commitment, one of the crucial tests of modern reform is the extent to which educational opportunities have been provided to all groups of people. In the United States, the fact that certain groups—such as women, blacks, and Hispanics—seemed to be consistently discriminated against both within the schools and outside them gives pause to the claim that American schools have adequately served the ideal of equal opportunity.

These failings have been explained in a number of ways, and each of these explanations has had somewhat different implications for educational policy. There are three explanations that we want to explore here,[1] each of which has been associated with a certain attitude toward educational reform. One is a politically liberal response and the other two are conservative. The first of these explanations, the liberal one, we will call

29

the historical impediments argument; the second and third will be called the intellectual impediments and the cultural impediments arguments, respectively. While these three explanations differ among themselves in respect to issues related to equality of educational opportunity, they are all reasonably consistent with a functionalist point of view. By exploring them in some detail, we will be able to see some of the various uses to which functionalist thinking may be put. As an introduction to some of the issues raised in this chapter, you might want to consider the case "College or Workforce?" in chapter 8.

Historical Impediments and Compensatory Education

Advocates of the historical impediments argument claim that minorities do not lack talent but rather have suffered long periods of discrimination by the dominant majority. They conclude that the present generation of minority children is due extra assistance. Thus, the historical impediments argument has been associated with federally supported compensatory educational programs such as Project Head Start and the Upward Bound program, which were initiated in the 1960s. The idea behind the Head Start program was to enable youngsters from poor and minority groups to become better prepared for public school by participating in preschool enrichment programs that would enhance their readiness for school. The Upward Bound program was directed at high-school youngsters from these same groups. Its intent was to help them make up deficiencies and thus better enable them to compete for admission to the nation's colleges and universities. Other programs, such as the Educational Opportunities Program, operated at the college level. In this program, promising youth from underrepresented minority groups were sought out for admission under more flexible admissions criteria. In some cases a special curriculum was designed for such young people in order to improve their ability to compete in standard college courses.

Those who adopt the historical impediments argument tend to look upon the underrepresentation of minority groups in higher education and the better-paying occupations as a social problem whose correction requires a large political and economic commitment. They accept the general goal of equal opportunity, and they believe that the schools have been effective in helping a large number of individuals achieve this goal. However, they tend to view the underachievement of certain ethnic, racial, or sexual groups as a sign of a specific handicap, such as economic or cultural deprivation, that has been brought about by social prejudice or historical injustice, such as slavery. They thus argue that true equality of opportunity requires that the schools compensate for this handicap. In other words, equality of opportunity requires equality of *educational* opportunity.

The nature of the compensation advocated takes different forms. If the impediment is perceived as one in which the child's parents speak a different language or dialect from the one used in school, then some form of bilingual education might be proposed. If the problem is perceived to be that women have been socialized to view mathematics with fear and anxiety, then compensation may involve therapeutic programs designed to eliminate such anxiety. If the problem is seen to arise from cultural and intellectual impediments brought about by extreme poverty, compensatory programs might provide the materials and experiences that will serve to overcome these deficiencies.

These compensatory programs have often been justified on the strictly ethical ground that fairness dictates that handicaps be compensated if a just society is to be achieved. Yet, as we have seen, this ethical view also fits well into the functionalist understanding of modern society, where the expansion of schooling and the development of more effective means for identifying talent are explained by the new skills required by an ever more complex technology. In other words, by striving to compensate for certain handicaps, we are not just improving the lot of individuals; we are benefiting the society as a whole. Thus, two goods, the individual's and the society's, are being pursued simultaneously.

This kind of justification for compensatory programs represents the liberal development of the functionalist position. Not everyone has been satisfied with the results of compensatory programs, and a conservative reaction has emerged. Like its liberal counterpart, this reaction is supported by and is compatible with many features of functionalist theory. However, instead of supporting most of the compensatory programs that have been initiated in recent years, it opposes or seeks to modify them in important ways.

Intellectual and Cultural Impediments

Two kinds of objections to the historical impediments model have been expressed. The first argues that while historical discrimination may have some effect on school performance, it is relatively small. The more important factor is the natural ability that people are born with. Compensatory programs will not be able to close the gap in intelligence, because this gap arises from differences in natural endowment. Compensatory programs can change only environmental factors. This argument is the intellectual impediments argument. Its advocates believe that IQ tests are reasonably accurate measures of native intelligence. Evidence drawn from scores on such tests is used to support the view that, on the average, different groups are genetically endowed with different intellectual capacities, which, for some groups, limit their ability to profit from programs intended to improve general intelligence.

The cultural impediments argument places much less emphasis on natural ability and native intelligence. Much like the advocates of the historical impediments argument, its proponents see the most important factor in achievement to be environmental, and especially cultural. However, instead of viewing this factor as external to the individual and alterable by an act of political will, culture is viewed as resistant to political manipulation from external institutions such as schools. Culture and family background are seen to place strong limits on a child's motivation and hence on the individual's willingness to accept the discipline that the school requires. The advocates of both the intellectual and the cultural impediments arguments reject the view that differences in achievement across different cultural, racial, or sexual groups provide sufficient evidence to claim that the principle of equality of opportunity is being violated. They argue that other factors are at work.

The intellectual impediments model stresses the view that individuals differ with regard to their abstract conceptual ability. Its advocates observe that the principle of equality of opportunity only requires that such differences be fairly and accurately appraised and that people with similar ability be treated in similar ways. Moreover, advocates of this model believe that it is likely that the average intelligence of some groups will be higher than that of others. They conclude that if this is the case, then an unequal distribution of achievement and rewards will be consistent with the principle of equality of opportunity.

Advocates of the intellectual impediments model believe that it is possible to measure objectively the general intelligence of different individuals through the use of standardized and "culture-fair" tests designed for this purpose. Others do not agree. Nevertheless, IQ tests have been used and justified on the grounds that they can best predict the achievement potential of an individual child. Researchers such as Herrnstein and Murray have argued that because average IQ test scores of certain groups, such as African Americans, are consistently below those of other groups, such as whites and Asian Americans, it is likely that there is a real, genetically determined difference in intellectual ability among members of these groups. Herrnstein and Murray suggest that the difference in both achievement and social rewards that we find is likely the result of differences in intellectual ability and that it is unlikely that these differences are a sign that the principle of equality of opportunity is being violated on a large scale.[2] Serious challenges to this argument have been made on a number of grounds. Some argue that IQ is too narrow a concept and that human intelligence takes many different forms. Others argue that IQ tests, even so-called "culture-fair" ones, are biased towards white middle class culture, and some geneticists reject the whole idea that black people and white people constitute two biologically separate groups. Still others note the way in which the ideology of IQ ignores the different experiences of black people and white people in a racist society.

In contrast to those who argue the case for the intellectual impediments model, advocates of the cultural impediments model take the criticism of IQ tests seriously. They deny that intelligence, as measured by an IQ test, is really an adequate explanation for the different levels of achievement that are found among members of different racial and ethnic groups. To support this view, they point to a number of studies that have succeeded in raising IQ scores significantly. Those who advance this position argue that motivational factors are much more important in explaining differential achievement and rewards than is measured IQ. Motivational factors are seen to be closely tied to factors of family life and culture.

According to one of the staunchest advocates of the cultural impediments model, Edward Banfield,[3] motivation is the primary factor in achievement, but high or low levels of motivation are best understood in terms of an individual's ability to conceptualize space and time, to project himself or herself into a distant future and a wider community, and to discipline present resources toward future ends. Variations in such ability are the defining characteristics of what Banfield calls "class culture." On one end of the scale we have the upper class, which is said to be marked by a strong sense of altruism, to be able to project itself into a far and distant future in time, to identify with the world community as a whole, and to discipline present wants toward long-term, future ends. At the other extreme, according to Banfield, is the lower class, which lives from moment to moment, identifies only with the self as it exists in the here and now, and is prone to violence. In between these two extremes lie the middle and the working classes: the one able to identify with the future of their children and with a local, state, or national community; the other able to conform to the routine required to meet short-term needs and to identify only with family and friends.

Banfield rejects the idea that people's orientation toward space and time is transmitted through the genes of their parents. Rather, they are transmitted subtly through the features of everyday life that characterize the activities of a given class culture. For example, the behavior of different families at mealtime provides an occasion in which the essential features of class may be transmitted from one generation to the next.

Some families may insist upon a formal dinner, with each child waiting his or her turn to eat, talk, or serve. Others may engage in a free-for-all, where each member struggles with every other member for food, conversation, or time and where, at the end of the meal, the clutter is left behind. In still other families mealtime may be a very lonely affair, where, when hungry, each member seeks gratification without hope of company or companionship. These examples provide some idea of the intricate complexities that are involved in the transmission of a class culture orientation as Banfield and other advocates of the cultural impediments model perceive it. More important, however, these examples provide a sense of the difficulties that advocates of this position believe are involved in trying to change a person's cultural orientation. Any kind of state intervention intended to alter the mealtime behavior of a family would be seen by the advocates of this view as an intolerable violation of the rights of privacy.

There are some points of similarity between the historical and the cultural impediments models. The implications drawn from these points, however, are quite different. Those who argue the case for historical impediments are quite willing to grant that factors of culture may have a strong influence on school achievement. However, they look to some historical pattern of events as molding the features of a local culture, and they argue that institutional change, especially change in schools, can bring about positive changes in the culture. In contrast, those who advocate the cultural impediments model will tend to minimize the extent to which the public school can be an effective instrument for social change. Since achievement is largely a function of class culture and since it is believed that little can be done to alter behavior that is rooted in class culture, they conclude that we can expect little significant impact from compensatory programs. Indeed, they believe that schools may make matters worse by trying to change the social standing of individuals. According to this view it is difficult to raise social class standing through the intervention of formal institutions. However, it is less difficult to lower it. When schools attempt to cater to the lower classes, the result is too often that the entire curriculum is watered down and the standards for achievement are relaxed for everybody. Banfield argues that a more functional program might be to provide opportunities and incentives for working-class youngsters to leave school and enter the world of work at an earlier age. Recognizing that little can be done for the lower-class child, this policy would at least provide working-class children with immediate monetary rewards and the discipline that comes from the world of work. In the meantime, public schools could re-establish their academic standards and thereby truly educate the children of the middle and upper classes.

Poverty

Functionalists seek to explain changes in schools and other social practices as rational adaptations to changing social needs. Some cultural impediments theorists have also attempted to explain urban poverty in this same way. They argue that the growth and vitality of cities will produce a poorer class of people, often recent migrants, who will occupy the more dilapidated houses in the inner city, work in the lowest-paying jobs, and send their children to the most run-down schools, while those who came earlier move up in jobs and out away from the city's core. Thus, the impoverished condition of a group of people at a certain point in time is seen as an inevitable aspect of contemporary society. It is the price that is paid for progress. Banfield, for example, takes this position, which he describes as the inevitable "logic" of metropolitan growth.[4]

This concept is intended to provide us with a long-range perspective through which we may better understand poverty. While individual mobility, especially among members of newer groups, may not always be apparent, this concept tells us that we have reason to expect that there will be improvement from one generation to the next. For example, we should find that the children of immigrants are better off than their parents. In those instances where this is not the case and where the situation of the child is the same as or worse than that of the parent, the cultural impediments model directs us to look at the internal workings of the family or the local culture to explain the lack of progress.[5] However, this perspective complicates the issues raised by the principle of equality of opportunity. In judging whether equality of opportunity is operative in any given society, we must now not only judge talent and motivation on the one side against rewards on the other, we must also calculate such factors as when a group arrived in an area and the rate of urban growth.

Some would argue that when carried this far, the cultural impediments model has implicitly and for all practical purposes abandoned equality of opportunity as an operating principle for contemporary society. In denying that education is likely to effect significant change and provide opportunities that would otherwise be denied, it seems to provide an argument that allows existing inequalities to persist unaddressed. Furthermore, by insisting that inequality be seen as simply the natural outgrowth of urban development, it allows little room for judging any large-scale inequality as inappropriate and therefore undercuts the distinction between natural and accidental inequality upon which the principle of equal opportunity rests. Thus, in attempting to explain inequality, the argument has the effect of denying its significance. In so doing, the cultural impediments model seems unwittingly to deny the importance of the one principle that was thought crucial for distinguishing modern from traditional societies, that of equality of opportunity. Talent and motivation may count in deciding one's placement in advanced, industrial society, but they do not count as much as the moment at which one's cultural group or family enters a growing society. In effect, the cultural impediments model seems to provide an argument for doing little to correct for disadvantages in order to encourage the realization of equal opportunity.

Problems with Functionalism

Functionalists believe that they have developed a scientific undertanding of social life. They believe that functionalism provides an objective, nonideological theory for analyzing the reasons for and the effects of existing social institutions and practices. Some critics of functionalism argue that the theory is not neutrally objective and scientific. Some even view it as an ideological weapon that provides an unwarranted justification for the institutions and practices of modern society. Some see it as politically conservative. In this concluding section, we want to look at some of these criticisms of functionalism, explore the functionalists' response to their critics, and stimulate you to make your own appraisal of functionalism. First, we turn to the question of whether functionalism has an inherently conservative bias. Since this is a criticism that has been addressed by some strong advocates of functionalism, it will be useful to look first at their own attempts to address the issue of political bias.

One of the most significant criticisms of functionalism has been developed by Robert K. Merton, who is himself an important contemporary advocate of functionalism. Merton acknowledges the fact that because many functionalists have assumed that every social practice and institution must be understood in terms of its adaptive function for the society as a whole, they have tended to give a primary value to existing social forms. Thus he grants that functionalist scholarship often has had a conservative tone.

Merton, however, is especially critical of those forms of functionalism that tend to examine a cultural institution and "to single out only the apparently integrative consequences and to neglect its possible disintegrative consequences."[6] Arguing against the view that every specific custom, practice, or belief system must fulfill some vital function for the society in which it is found, he suggests instead that our understanding of a society is better served by "the provisional assumption that persisting cultural forms have a *net balance of functional consequences.*"[7] This will help us to realize that there are many times when existing practices may be taking "the place of more effective alternatives."[8] For example, to the extent that schools have contributed to the continuation of racism or sexism in modern society, it would seem that they have served a disintegrative function. By remaining open to such possibilities, functionalism can, according to Merton, serve as a refined, nonideological tool for social change. It can suggest alternative institutions and practices.

It remains to be seen whether or not Merton has successfully addressed the problem of the conservative political bias of functionalism. However, before we return to look at this issue, we need to examine an important conceptual problem that Merton has also tried to solve. This is the problem of how a function is to be identified. For example, how do we distinguish a function from the motives that individuals may have for participating in an institution or engaging in a practice? Consider Dreeben's analysis of schooling in order to see the problem.

Dreeben tells us that the essential function of schooling in modern society is to teach the norms required for life in a meritocratic world. Yet this is only one reason why people participate in and support public schools. There are many others. For example, some parents find the school to be a convenient baby-sitting service; some teachers depend upon the school for their income; some students find it to be a congenial social setting; some labor leaders feel that schools help to control what would otherwise be an oversupply of workers; and some business leaders believe that schooling is an effective way of developing a skilled workforce. Given all of these different reasons for supporting schools, how do we determine that some of them are to be identified as "functions" while others are not?

Merton believes that he has an answer to this question. He tells us that functions "are those observed consequences which make for the adaptation or adjustment of a given system."[9] Functions thus refer to adaptive social consequences, while reasons and motives are presumably associated only with individual wants. Reasons and motives may coincide with the functions of an institution, but then again they may not. According to Merton, an institution may serve certain critical social functions even without anyone consciously willing that those functions be served.

Given Merton's distinction between functions and reasons, it would seem that the use of schools to establish the norms required to work and to live in a meritocratic society is to be taken as a "function" because it serves the adaptive needs of the social system. It would appear that using the schools as an expensive baby-sitting agency, however, would be classified as an individual motive because it does not seem to serve the society's adaptive needs. Yet is the distinction as clear-cut as it might seem? Clearly the schools' function as a baby-sitting agency often frees parents from the home and allows them to work outside of it. It also enables single parents to leave their children for long periods during the day to find work. Modern society seems to encourage parents to work outside of the home, and thus it seems reasonable to view the baby-sitting function of schooling as a social adaptation. In this instance, there is no clear-cut way to distinguish a function in Merton's terms from a motive.

While the distinction between functions and motives is not as clear-cut as Merton suggests, the really important issue for him is whether a function must be consciously recognized by the social participants themselves—whether a function is "manifest" or "latent." His concern is to establish an objective understanding of society that is not dependent upon the subjective recognition of its participants.

A *manifest function* is one that is intended and recognized by members of the social system themselves. A *latent function* is one that serves the adaptive needs of the society but that is not intended or recognized by its members. The distinction between manifest and latent functions is an important one. If successful, it will enable functionalists to carry out their analysis of social institutions without relying on the stated reasons or motives of the social actors. But how many people need to be aware of the adaptive role of a function in order for it to be properly called a "manifest function"? Is the awareness of one person sufficient? Do we require a majority? Must all the members of a society be aware of it? Anthony Giddens raises this point in a criticism of Merton when he writes:

> Merton does not specify *who* has to intend and know what the function of an item is for it to be a manifest function. . . . The circumstances may easily exist in which some participants in a social system know what the functional consequences of others are, and where the others themselves are ignorant of such consequences. The significance of such a situation is not hard to see; it is likely to contribute to and express the power of those who are in the know over those who are not.[10]

It is unlikely that functionalists would accept Giddens's criticism. They would respond that a function can be manifest for some people and latent for others. However, the question of the relationship between social functions and individual motives leads Giddens to develop a more powerful criticism. He relates the functionalists' concern to minimize the role that purposeful human action has in the explanation of social events to the issue of causal explanation. His point is that there can be no explanation of social need that does not presuppose some individual want as part of the causal explanation.

In order to see this point, consider two standard, but somewhat contrasting, models of a causal explanation. In the first, suppose that your car tire suddenly goes flat and you notice that there is a nail in the tire. You thus explain the flat tire by noting that you must have run over the nail. This is a fairly standard kind of causal explanation. In this case you assume that first a certain event occurred (driving over the nail) that then had a certain effect (the tire went flat). Here the cause comes first and its consequence then follows.

Now consider a contrasting case. Upon leaving a store you are asked, "Why did you go into that store?" You answer, "Because I wanted to buy a loaf of bread." In this case the consequence of the action (buying the bread) has become a part of its cause. This is the kind of explanation that seems to characterize the functionalist idea. For example, to say that "schools exist because they develop the norms required by modern society" is to make the consequence part of the cause.[11] However, there is one important difference between the example of buying the bread and the functionalist view of explanation. In the bread example, the agent's wants were the mediating factor between the act of entering the store and the causal consequence of buying the bread. In the school example there is no agent. In other words, functionalists leave little role for individual wants.

Where human wants are present, explanations that make the consequence a part of the cause do not present any obvious problems. The difficulty with a functionalist explanation, at least as Giddens sees it, is that it makes the consequence a part of the cause but minimizes the importance of individual wants.[12] Thus when functionalists try to understand a certain institution by examining the contribution it makes to the survival and adaptation of the society in which it is found, they are seeking an explanation in which the consequences are a part of the cause. However, their explanation does not require that there be an individual or group that must intend those consequences.

This problem has led Giddens to suggest that the driving force behind functional explanations is the notion of some kind of system need that takes the place of individual wants. However, he finds this notion inappropriate. He writes: "Social systems, unlike organisms, do not have any need or interest in their own survival, and the notion of 'need' is falsely applied if it is not acknowledged that system needs presuppose actors' wants."[13] Giddens is not denying that certain individuals and groups will have an interest in the survival of a certain institution or practice. He is simply rejecting the idea that the system itself can have any such interest. Systems are not people, and therefore they do not have interests. Giddens's comments are important. A functionalist analysis often tends to depersonalize social movements, while attempting to view them in neutral, nonpolitical terms. Giddens's criticism is a reminder of the personal and political factors that must be taken into account in understanding social practice and institutional life.

Having now examined some of the conceptual problems that have been raised by functionalism's critics, we can return to reconsider the political criticism that was raised earlier and that Merton attempted to address. This is the question of whether functionalism is an inherently conservative theory, or, more specifically, whether it provides an uncritical acceptance of the institutions of modern society. Critics like Giddens view the attempt to depersonalize social decisions and institutions as an important feature of any version of functionalism. To these critics functionalism serves to hide the power relations that are to be found in modern Western society. They believe that by concealing these relations, functionalism has been an important instrument in maintaining them. In this way functionalism is taken to be not only politically conservative but also repressive. It is to this point of view that we turn in the next chapter.

Before going on, you might want to look at the dispute over "Individual Differences and Equal Opportunity" in chapter 8. To provide an introduction to Part III, the dispute over "Social Reproduction" may be useful.

Part III

SCHOOLING
AS LEGITIMATION
AND REPRODUCTION

Chapter 4

Marxist Theory and Education

Conflict Theory and Functionalism

We have seen that functionalists believe that the driving force behind the expansion of schooling is the need created by a highly industrialized, modern society to develop the skills and attitudes that are appropriate for a changing economic and social world. Functionalists like Dreeben argue that the modern school furthers the selection of individuals on the basis of merit and talent and, in so doing, discourages the distribution of income, social positions, and authority on the basis of family background, race, sex, or religion. Thus, for the functionalist, schools serve both a social and an individual purpose. On the social level they help assure that the skills and attitudes required by an industrial, urban democracy will be developed and maintained. On the individual level, they enhance the possibility that placement into jobs and the distribution of income, prestige, and authority will be fair.

While functionalism has been the dominant tradition in educational scholarship and research, it has not been without competitors. Among these, conflict theory has been the most prominent. Conflict theory derives from a number of sources. Marxist scholarship is clearly the most influential and the one that we will address most fully.

Whereas functionalists believe that the driving force behind social and educational change is the progressive movement toward technical development and social integration, conflict theorists believe the driving force in complex societies is the unending struggle between different groups to hold power and status. In modern society, they see schools as an important instrument in this struggle. They believe that schools serve the dominant privileged class by providing for the social reproduction of the economic and political status quo in a way that gives the illusion of objectivity, neutrality, and opportunity. They believe that the schools reproduce the attitudes and dispositions that are required for the continuation of the present system of domination by the privileged class.

Even though the groups that are visibly contesting for power may differ from time to time, Marxist-orientated conflict theorists believe that the basic cause of such conflict can usually be traced to differences among social classes. Thus, the direct conflict may be one among blacks and whites, males and females, or Christians and Jews, but the underlying cause will be found in something deeper—the division between the classes in a capitalist society. One important implication of this view is that while the deeper reason for a conflict involves class differences, the participants themselves may view the struggle as essentially racial, ethnic, generational, or sexual. Another implication is that there may be times when no struggle is visible and even the participants believe that harmony reigns. Yet on closer examination the seeds of conflict become visible to an outside observer. We will return to look at these and other implications shortly. First, however, it will be useful to see the different ways in which functionalism and conflict theory might view the same event.

Imagine that you are the dean of a college of education within a large state university, and you decide to increase the standards for entrance into your program. In this imaginary world, the degree in education has recently become one of the more lucrative credentials that the university is providing. Thus, your program has attracted an increasing number of applicants, and you have good evidence for believing that standards can be raised significantly without reducing the number of students entering the program. This calculation is important because the amount of resources that your school receives from the total university is partly determined by the number of students in the program. In addition, however, the university is concerned about the ranking of the teacher education program nationally, and there is a good chance that by increasing standards the national ranking of the college of education will improve. Moreover, colleges of education from other universities have been increasing their entrance standards, and unless similar steps are taken by your college, it will likely lose ground in the national rankings. An additional incentive for raising entrance standards is the competitive edge that a higher national ranking will provide your students in bidding for the better jobs in the best schools. Hence, from your own point of view, there is an overwhelming set of interrelated reasons for raising standards. To do so will enhance the position of your college within the university and will allow stronger arguments to be made for increasing your budget. At the same time a higher budget will allow you to hire more prestigious faculty, who will increase the attractiveness of your teacher education program for the better students. With both better faculty and better students, the national ranking of your program will continue to improve, and employers will be more likely to hire students from your institution than those from competing ones.

From the functionalist point of view, the important things to see in this process are the way it actually serves to increase the talent and the technical skills that are available to the public school community and the fact that this is accomplished by instituting standards that can be applied universally to any and all applicants. Raising standards means increasing the institution's ability to discriminate on the basis of relevant criteria alone. Lower standards mean more eligible applicants and therefore more room for judgments made on the basis of less relevant factors such as in-state/out-of-state discrimination, sex, and minority quotas.

From the point of view of the conflict theorists, the situation may look quite different. They might see the result of higher standards working this way: In order to meet the new admissions requirements that have been established, students from outstanding secondary schools would clearly have the edge over those whose schools are less adequate. Since the most outstanding secondary schools are found in wealthy communities where the citizens can afford the price of high-quality education, the children of the wealthy will clearly have a marked advantage. Moreover, if a required course of study is missing from a high-school curriculum, or if a child is having difficulty with a certain subject, wealthy parents can afford to provide outside help and tutoring. Poorer parents cannot usually afford to provide this kind of help, and their children are almost completely dependent on what the public school has to offer. Thus, to raise standards for admission into the college of education is to place an added burden on the already disadvantaged. While the intent of the reform is simply to raise standards and to provide a competitive advantage to the college and its students, the effect, as seen from the conflict theorists' point of view, is to reduce the opportunities for the less advantaged youngster and to increase opportunities for the more advantaged one.

This example can be used to point out some important features of the conflict theory model. First, there is no necessary and direct relation between the intent behind an action or policy and the social effects of that action. In this case the intent of the dean was to raise standards and to increase the competitive advantage of students in the college of education. It was neither to decrease the opportunities for the less wealthy students nor to increase them for the more wealthy students. While there may be some cases in which a college policy is instituted with these goals in mind, they may also come about as the unintended consequences of other, more acceptable motives. Second, because the social effects may arise without conscious intent, there is no need to suggest that they are the result of conspiratorial action. In this case, raising entrance standards benefited the already advantaged wealthy students. It also improved the already admirable position of the college of education. It even promised benefits to the affluent schooling community, which will get more talented teachers. However, there is no reason to believe that some conscious plan or plot has been devised in order to achieve these goals. In other words, it is possible to have a system in which different members of an advantaged class decide matters independently of one another without intentionally serving the narrow interest of their own class.

The problem with functionalism, according to conflict theory, is that, consciously or not, it takes the interests and perspectives of the dominant social groups in society and elevates them to the status of universal norms. Having done this, it then uses these norms to measure the contributions of members of all other groups. In this way the interests of a particular class are misrepresented as belonging to the society as a whole, and this misrepresentation then serves to maintain the privileged position of the members of that class. In our example, certain forms of achievement, which are the values of prestigious universities and affluent school systems, become the universalized norm that keeps other groups out of teaching and maintains the affluent in the best positions. This criticism of functionalism has been developed most explicitly by that form of conflict theory known as Marxism, and it is to that perspective that we now turn. Before going on, you may want to consider the case "Equal but Separate" in chapter 8.

Marxist Theory

In order to understand Marxism, it is essential to grasp a fundamental idea about the relationship between the way we think and the way we live. For the Marxist, the way people think, perceive, and feel—that is, their "consciousness"—is related to the basic mode of economic production in their society. This means that people's fundamental ideas about the nature of truth and falsity, about goodness and beauty, can be understood by examining the way in which production is carried on at a certain point in time. It is important not to confuse Marxism with relativism, a position that we will examine briefly in the next chapter. Marxists are not arguing, as the relativists do, that what is true, good, or beautiful is whatever I or my culture takes to be truth, goodness, or beauty. Rather they believe that the basic concepts by which we organize our conceptual, ethical, and aesthetic worlds can be understood only if we recognize their relation to the productive possibilities of the society in which we live.

To illustrate, let us consider two of the fundamental categories through which we organize our physical world, those of *space* and *time*. These categories are a part of our "consciousness" and are fundamental to any truth claims we might make, since they allow us to locate objects and events in a way that would otherwise be impossible. Indeed, it is the conceptions of space and time that make much of our everyday conversation intelligible. If I say, "It is raining outside," or "Sally is depressed today," or "School was closed during the summer," what I am saying can be understood and its truth or falsity determined only because I share with my listener implicit conceptions of space and time. We both divide time into the same units, for example, day and night, summer and winter; and we divide space in similar ways, for example, inside and outside.

Thus, conceptions of space and time seem to be conditions for intelligibility and mutual understanding in any human society. This insight is not unique to Marxist theory. Interpretivists would also hold this view. The unique contribution of Marxist theory can be seen when we look at specific conceptions that different groups have of space and time. Take the idea of space. In our own civilization, we will often locate objects in space by using specific coordinates such as north, east, south, and west. So if it is said that "New York is south of Boston," the statement is both understandable and true. It is understandable because we each share the conception of direction, which includes the coordinates north, east, south, and west. And it is true because, given this understanding, New York is in fact south of Boston. It is important, however, to see that being "south of" indicates a relationship. To tell someone to go south is not like telling them to go to New York. The first involves an abstract notion of space, while the latter notion is concrete. There is a concrete place "New York"; "south" is not such a place.

Now imagine a society that has not yet invented the abstract concepts north, east, south, and west. Perhaps this would be a society in which directions would be given only in terms of local concrete objects: "Go to the big rock"; "look for the river"; "follow the stream"; "at the fork, look for the biggest tree"; and so forth. Here the statement that one place is south of another would be neither true nor false. It would have no meaning at all.

Truth for the Marxist is not relative in the sense that anything that one's culture deems true is true. Rather, truth is dependent on the concepts that one's culture makes available. At any given stage of our culture's development, certain concepts are made available to us that then allow us to think in new ways; and education plays a large role in ensuring that we come to share our culture's most important concepts. Now the question to be asked is: Just how do concepts such as north, east, south, and west arise? or How can we account for their development? One possible answer is that they are the inventions of very talented individuals who are able to break away from the limited forms of thought that their own civilization provides and invent new ones. The problem with this view is that it does not tell us what it is that allows such people to break the traditional boundaries of thinking (something that is very hard to do), or why the concepts of some talented people may be accepted at a certain time and become ingrained in the thinking of the population as a whole while the conceptual inventions of others are rejected.

For the Marxist, the way to address these questions properly is to explore the relationship between changes in the mode of production and changes in the characteristics of thought. In essence, the Marxist is asking us to break the traditional boundaries of our thinking and look at a new conception of how concepts and "consciousness" are formed. Let us return to our hypothetical example of the development from a concrete conception of space to an abstract one. Suppose we were to ask which was better, the concrete conception of space, where individuals are extraordinarily sensitive to immediate visual cues, or the abstract conception of space, which allows unknown areas to be charted and traveled. Given our own modern framework, where the abstract conception of space has become taken for granted and serves as an important tool, there would be little hesitation in answering the question.

Assume, however, that the material needs of the members of the earlier culture in our example are easily met; that people live quite happily and peacefully in a lush, isolated, self-contained area. Food, shelter, and other necessary items are available within the boundaries that their concrete understanding of space allows them to travel. Assume, too, that the use of a more sophisticated, abstract, and flexible notion of space could bring this group into areas where it would find itself in conflict with other groups. Given these assumptions, it is difficult to proclaim categorically that the more sophisticated conception of spatial relations is a better conception than the less sophisticated one.

Suppose, however, that certain key resources become scarce or that the environment is no longer sufficient to support a growing population. If the group is to continue to survive, means must be developed to go far afield to find new resources. Some of these means might be material ones, such as larger, more durable boats or suitable overland conveyances that could bring back the needed resources. Others would be conceptual. New ways of locating one's position in earthly space would be important to be able to travel and return successfully. The group might even invent north, east, south, and west! "Necessity is the mother of invention," but for the Marxist this does not just mean material inventions; it means conceptual ones as well, and such "inventions" are stimulated by changes in our material conditions. Therefore to say whether one way of conceiving of space is better than another way, we have to be able to view it in relation to existing material conditions and needs of a certain historical period.

While the example illustrates how conceptual differences might evolve historically within a group, it does not provide a sense of the different ways of thinking that can be found among different groups existing within the same society during the same historical period. Marxists explain this by using the concept of social class. For the Marxist, whenever people are related in different ways to the means of production we have a class society, and each particular class is defined in terms of this relationship. For example, in a capitalist society, where the means of production are privately owned, the group that owns them will constitute a different class from the group that is hired to work in their factories and plants. As we shall see, being a member of a class will entail many things that go well beyond the relation that one has to the means of production. It will entail having certain values, a certain outlook, and a set of perceptions and concepts about the nature of social life, or, in sum, having a certain "class consciousness."

Class Consciousness, False Consciousness, and Hegemony

According to Marxism, a class can exist in two different ways—*objectively* and *subjectively*. Objectively, all of those people who must sell their labor to others in order to meet their daily needs and who do not own any significant part of the production process may be thought of as a class—the working class. Since a class is defined only in terms of the relation its members have to the means of production, a class may consist of many different kinds of individuals. For example, the working class contains people of different races, nationalities, and religions. However, because of their differences, they may fail to recognize their working-class interest as a shared one. In this instance the class would be said to have an objective existence but to lack consciousness of itself as a class. If the members of a class become aware of their common interest and are able to articulate that interest through common action and through legitimate spokespeople, then the class has not only an objective existence but also a subjective existence. At this stage it has become conscious of itself as a class. The labor union movement is sometimes an example of this. Its existence is reflected in the subjective understanding of its members. And it may be able to exert its collective power for its own interests.

The development of class consciousness may be blocked by society, and progressive social change may be impeded. Marxists use the concepts of *false consciousness* and *hegemony* to explain how this can happen. Members of the subordinate class who express the point of view and share the values of the dominant class exhibit false consciousness. True consciousness of your own class is impeded by your acceptance of the values of the dominant class. When the dominant class is successful in establishing its own mode of thinking among most members of the subordinate class, it is said to have established hegemony over the subordinate class. Hegemony means having a preponderance of influence and authority over others. This influence is expressed both in the concepts and the institutional arrangements of the social structure. False consciousness is illustrated by the slave who espouses the values of the master. The slave believes that he or she is the master's property, to do with as the master pleases. It is also illustrated by the worker who carries the values of the owner or by the concentration camp inmate who begins to think like the prison guard. Hegemony exists when one class controls the thinking of another class through such cultural forms as the media, the church, or the schools.

Orthodox Marxists believe that all social change, including changes in the way in which we think about the world around us, is rooted in the way in which people produce their goods and in the possibilities that new productive methods open up for positive human development. This means that the political, legal, religious, and educational systems must be understood dynamically in terms of whether, in any given historical period, they serve to enhance or to hinder human development. Thus, a system that, at one point in time, may have served a progressive role in a society may, because of changes in the possibilities created by new modes of production, come to serve a negative function. This means that it may be quite appropriate and functional for a certain perspective or ideology to dominate thinking at a given historical moment, while at a later time those same ideas may become unproductive expressions of false consciousness and hegemony. Let us consider a case in order to illustrate this.

Imagine a society, not unlike those in Western Europe during the Middle Ages, where there are strong moral, religious, and legal sanctions against the practice of usury, that is, the charging of high interest rates for loans. Let us assume that this society does not have the means to accumulate capital or material goods and cannot store food and other perishable necessities for long periods of time. The production and consumption of necessities are tightly bound together in an agrarian life style. At this point in time the restrictions against usury make sense, because there is little possibility for economic growth and because the upward mobility of one person would mean the downward mobility of another. In other words, since little possibility for economic growth exists, the mutual well-being of all depends upon a smooth and stable relationship among different segments of the society. At this stage money lending is not very common, but when it occurs it is usually performed as an act of friendship. It serves to cement essential communal relations. Usury threatens to destroy those relations by turning friendship into a business. However, because there is a recognition that certain unforeseen disasters may require larger sums of money than friends can afford to lend, a special group is designated as the money-lenders-of-last-resort. These people are defined as outside of the community and generally looked down upon. The moral code that governs the members of the dominant community pictures a world of mutual service where God has given each member a specific place and role.

Suppose, however, that at another point in time new possibilities arise in the form of new knowledge about production and navigation, possibilities that, if realized, will increase the total wealth available to all. These possibilities could occur in a number of areas all at once. They might include new methods for storing food, new techniques for navigating long distances, and new ways of building larger and sturdier ships that are able to cross oceans and bring back spices to preserve foods, new kinds of fiber, gold, and exotic material goods. However, to bring these possibilities about and to realize the new wealth that they will make possible, large stores of capital must be brought together and centralized under a single project. Borrowing now becomes more businesslike and necessary.

Now the restrictions against usury would stand as an impediment to the accumulation of new wealth, and strong arguments might be developed for their elimination. As usury laws are overturned, wealth would become more centralized; large, previously unthinkable projects could be undertaken; and new territories might then be discovered, providing even more incentive for the centralization of capital. This would lead to an increase in the physical and economic mobility of individuals, in a rapid growth of cities, in new political power for a new class of merchants, bankers, and manufacturers. Moreover, in order to assure the flow of materials from recently discovered territories, a governing structure attached to the homeland would have to be extended to these areas, and colonies would need to be established.

As control over different and strange people is extended, a different moral conception would be needed to justify these extended political structures. Writers might begin to develop new themes (such as the idea of the "white man's burden") for home consumption and legitimation of hegemony abroad. New educational forms would develop in order to maintain the flow of administrators needed to govern the foreign areas. Promising native students from the territories would have to be provided the opportunity to study in the homeland before returning to their own country to take up positions as subservient, middle-level administrators. And in the process, a new equilibrium would be developed between the society's productive capacities and the new social norms, legal regulations, and patterns of thought that have arisen because of the shift in relationships to the means of production.

Marxists observe that new codes are developed by and for a specific social class. They note that the development of a new code involves a struggle with other classes, which serve as the protective agents for the older, more established norms. In our example, new norms would be advanced by and for the manufacturing, banking, and merchant classes, while the older norms would be defended by the agrarian aristocracy and supported by the traditional elements of the clergy. In order to enlist the support of other classes, the new moral code would be advanced, not as serving the narrow interest of the rising classes, but as "universal principles" that promise to serve the interest of all. For example, in American history, the principles of "life, liberty, and the pursuit of happiness" were not explicitly articulated as serving the interests of only a specific class of people, even though the founding fathers had common interests as slave owners and large property holders. Rather, these ideals were formulated to appeal to as wide a range of individuals as possible. They were expressed as universal rights that would advance the position of everyone against what was seen by some as oppressive taxation and arbitrary rule by the monarchy. In general, this is a very good tactical move—it helps enlist the support of many dissatisfied elements in society. However, it also helps create a new set of standards by which even the emerging order and its newly advantaged classes may eventually be judged. In less than a hundred years a war over slavery was fought in the United States. Today freedom and equality are still elusive prizes for many blacks, other minority groups, and women.

Returning to our example, instead of a medieval society governed by the idea that God has given each and every person a specific place in life, we now would have a society in which people believed that talent should determine one's social and economic position. Of course, this principle is exactly the same as that expressed by the functionalists—that in modern society it is *achieved*, rather than *ascribed*, characteristics that are to be rewarded. However, the difference between the Marxists and the functionalists on this point must also be remembered. The functionalists believe that this principle serves as a *real* universal norm, one which evolved and governs the process of selection of talent in modern society. In contrast, the Marxists believe that the principle is best seen historically as a weapon in a class struggle used first to overcome one's assigned place in life and used later by the newly advantaged groups to maintain their gains and by the still disadvantaged ones to assert their claims to equal treatment.

Before continuing, you might want to look back at chapter 2's imaginary Third-World cases, where education for national purposes was used to illustrate the functionalist point of view. How would a Marxist interpret these cases? Is hegemony being exercised? Who would suffer from false consciousness? How would class separation be manifested?

Marxism, Neo-Marxism, and Education

There are at least two different opinions among Marxists about the role of social and educational research. Orthodox Marxists believe that their task is to discover instances of sciencelike laws that govern social movement. They believe that social research should seek to explain the way in which a particular mode of production (which includes both the means by which goods are produced and the relations of different classes to the means of production) influences and determines other forms of social life. In Marxist theory one of the fundamental laws has been the law of contradiction. This law holds that each social form contains within it the seeds of its own destruction and transcendence. In capitalist society, for example, there is an essential contradiction in the fact that while the means of production are privately owned, they are socially used. In other words, the means of production, such as factories and machinery, are owned by private individuals for their own profit, but the operation of this productive capacity requires a workforce of nonowners that is brought together in a common work place to work cooperatively. This creates the conditions required for the development of class consciousness among workers, whom the Marxists call the proletariat. With a disciplined, self-conscious proletarian work force that senses it is being exploited, the means are in place for seizing control of the productive forces and taking them from private hands through revolution. We do not need to go into detail about all of the steps that are supposed to be involved in this process. It is sufficient to note that this development and others like it in history are seen by orthodox Marxists to have the force of a natural law about them. Orthodox Marxists believe that each social form *must* have within it the seeds of its own destruction; otherwise basic social change would not occur and the class in power would continue to sequester and use their power forever. While there are few Marxists who continue to take such a rigid and deterministic view of social change today, there are many who believe that economics and the relationship of classes to the means of production must be given primacy in understanding other institutions, including the public schools.

Newer forms of Marxism offer a challenge to the deterministic view of the orthodox position. These new forms are concerned with issues related not only to economic oppression but also to domination by classes in noneconomic social forms. These neo-Marxists still consider economic domination important, but they do not believe that the end of private ownership of the means of production is a guarantee that class domination in all its forms will come to an end. In other words, these neo-Marxists believe that there is a need to analyze critically each situation of domination on its own terms, without presupposing that the cause of injustice or inequality will always be found in the same place. Some believe that in contemporary society domination is as likely to be found in the communication structures as in the economic ones. Therefore, as much attention may need to be paid to the control of information as to the control of production. They argue that the media and the schools are as important for a Marxist critique of society as are the economic institutions and the means of production.

In recent years there has been an increasing interest in Marxist theory and an increasing application of its insights to schooling. To a large extent this renewed interest in Marxism can be understood in terms of the inability of functionalism to explain adequately some of the social effects of schooling. Randall Collins (who does not identify himself as a Marxist but as a conflict sociologist) lists a number of the failures of functionalist theory in explaining the social effects of schooling. He notes that functionalists argue that the increase in technological sophistication within society accounts for the increasing number of years required in school. However, Collins finds only a very loose relationship between years of education and any increase in the technological sophistication demanded by the job market. In reviewing the literature on this subject, he concludes that "the educational level of the U.S. labor force has changed in excess of that which is necessary to keep up with the skill requirements of jobs."[1]

The plausibility of the functionalist claim that there is a strong relationship between the increased number of years required in school and the educational level required by the technological demands of work rests on the fact that during the very early stages of industrialization, the basic skills required by the work world did undergo a change. Whereas reading and simple arithmetic were not requirements for most jobs in a preindustrial society, they are required in an industrial one. Yet functionalists have extrapolated from the relation between education and industrialization at this early stage and assumed that it holds for all stages. They then conclude that knowledge of higher-level mathematics and science is required for work in high-tech industries. Collins finds that this conclusion is not justified by the evidence. While there is likely some continuing relationship between the increasing technical sophistication of some jobs and the educational requirements needed to hold them, there is little evidence suggesting that most jobs demand higher-level technical skills. If the real increase in the years of schooling cannot be explained by an increase in the technological skills needed in most jobs, then the explanation will have to be sought elsewhere. Collins's argument is supported by others. Harry Braverman, for example, presents strong evidence that the skills required for a large number of positions in society have actually decreased; owners and managers try to squeeze more profits out of an enterprise by routinizing as much of the work as they possibly can.[2] This routinization of labor then provides them more control over the workforce by allowing the substitution of one worker for another. Thus owners are no longer dependent upon the labor of any one person or group. Moreover, according to Collins, there is little evidence that, for most jobs, the more educated the workers are, the more productive they are.[3] In fact, the opposite might be true. More education might make one less tolerant of routine and monotonous work. The dispute "Education for Work" in chapter 8 is relevant here.

Functionalists argue that the newly industrializing Third-World countries need an expanded educational system to develop a workforce. Yet in many of these countries increased education seems to produce a larger unemployed urban population that is overeducated for the types of jobs available. Rather than being driven by the technical and economic needs of the society, the educational system seems to develop a momentum of its own, and the economy is unable to provide jobs for the number of educated workers that the school system produces. According to conflict theorists, the fact that functionalism cannot account for these problems suggests that a new understanding is required. Marxist theorists have attempted to provide it.

A Neo-Marxist Interpretation of Schooling in Capitalist Society

Public schools are state-run educational agencies. According to Marxists, they must therefore be understood in terms of the role that the state plays as the arm of the ruling class. Marxists believe that in a capitalist society, schools will serve to reproduce the relations of production that are essential to maintaining the dominance of the capitalist class. This means that schools will produce workers who are able to work at the different levels of the capitalist enterprise. They produce managers and janitors, as well as an array of people in between. How do the schools do this? The answer is critical to Marxist educational thought, because one criticism of functionalism is based on findings that schools are relatively minor instruments for developing the technical skills required by modern, industrial society. If the schools do not reproduce the relations of production by reproducing the skills that workers need to be laborers, then what is it that schools do reproduce?

To answer this question from a Marxist point of view, we need to see the different ways in which Marxists believe that the state serves the ruling class. One of these is obvious. Through the courts, the police, and the army, the state maintains a monopoly on repressive powers. The repressive features of the state are those that involve force or the threat of force and that can be used whenever there is a direct assault on established property relations. The repressive state apparatus has limited utility, however. Its effectiveness depends upon the willingness of workers who are not members of the ruling class to intervene on behalf of the dominant group. This willingness itself can be assured only if the functionaries who staff the courts, the army, and the police can be counted on to "have the right thoughts." If they cannot be counted on to believe that what they are doing is right and justifiable, there remains the uncomfortable possibility that they will turn their weapons in the wrong direction. To put it in Marxist terms, the development of false consciousness is an essential component of maintaining the capitalist state.

Repressive force is costly, however, and an exclusive reliance on the police and the army can provide an intolerable expense for any state. In addition, while repression can be reasonably effective in preventing a population from performing acts that are directed against the ruling class, it is much less effective in forcing people to act in ways that advance the interest of the ruling class. For example, "working to rule" or to the "letter of the contract" often provides workers with an effective way to protest a situation without triggering the release of repressive force. Enthusiasm and commitment cannot be legislated, even though these are important factors in maintaining a stable structure of domination.

Because the repressive apparatus of the state is not sufficient to maintain the interests of the ruling class, another mechanism is needed, and this is what Louis Althusser calls the Ideological State Apparatuses (ISAs).[4] The ISAs include the communications institutions, such as newspapers, radio, and television; the cultural institutions, such as art, literature, and sports; the religious institutions; the family; political parties; and trade unions. And, above all, the ISAs include the schools. The function of all of these institutions is to provide people with compelling reasons for doing that which they otherwise might not be inclined to do and which is essential for maintaining the current system of production relations and power.

Neo-Marxists view the schools in modern society as the most important of the ISAs. In order to understand the importance of schooling in this process, it will help to return to a fundamental claim of functionalism and see the way in which it both fits and does not fit the reality of contemporary life. That claim, you will recall, is that contemporary society exhibits a strong movement from a system of rewards based on ascribed status to one in which rewards are based on achieved status. In fact, functionalists see this movement as one of the essential features of modern society. However, a number of considerations seem to suggest that their perception is less than correct. Among these is the treatment that has been accorded to certain groups in contemporary Western societies. It is clear, for example, that in the United States, African Americans, Mexican Americans, and other minorities have not been treated in the same way as more established groups and that children from these minorities often suffer disadvantages purely because of their racial or ethnic status. In addition, in almost all advanced capitalist societies, women still function at a disadvantage simply because of their sex. The treatment of minorities and women provides strong reasons to question the functionalist view that modern society strives to reward achieved characteristics. Moreover, the steps that have been taken to correct these inequities have not arisen out of any inner tendency of advanced society. They have come from grassroots political action, from protests, sit downs, boycotts, strikes, and other such means.

The treatment of minority groups and women tells only part of the story. In analyzing data from white males in the United States, Samuel Bowles and Herbert Gintis found that economic success cannot be explained by intelligence as measured by IQ tests. An IQ-based meritocracy does not exist.[5] Moreover, they found no significant relationship between the trend toward equalizing the number of years of schooling of individuals and the equalization of income.[6] Studies like these, both in the United States and elsewhere, suggest that ascribed characteristics still play a prominent role in the distribution of economic rewards and social benefits.

However, even though the functionalist claim about the importance of achieved qualities does not hold up as a matter of fact, it does hold up as a matter of belief. In other words, people think that rewards *ought* to be distributed according to achievement and merit rather than according to family background, sex, or ethnic group. They believe that a system that does otherwise is unfair, and they judge the merits of their own social system on the basis of how well they *think* it is meeting this standard. Individuals who are unhappy with their lot in life will be more likely to endure their situation if they believe they have been given a fair chance than if they believe the cards were stacked against them. And most people believe that free public schooling gives them a fair and equal chance in life; that it is up to them. According to Bowles and Gintis and other Marxists, schools provide an important element of political stability by legitimizing existing inequalities. In other words, while the primary role of schooling under a capitalist system is to reproduce the relations of production, and thereby to reproduce the hierarchical, autocratic system of labor, it must also provide people with the belief that they have been given an equal chance to succeed. The case "Workforce School" in chapter 8 raises some relevant issues.

Chapter 5

The Hidden Curriculum Revisited

In our examination of functionalism, we saw that the concept of the "hidden curriculum" helped to explain the indirect ways in which schooling serves to socialize students into the values and norms of modern, industrial society. Such behaviors as waiting in line, scheduling activity according to clock time, competing for the teacher's attention, and working independently were each seen as important preparatory elements in learning to work in modern society. Marxists also affirm that schools develop the attitudes required for work in modern capitalist society. Yet there is an important difference between the functionalist and the Marxist views. Functionalists, in their attachment to the idea that schools advance the principle of equal opportunity, tend to assume that the curriculum is a fair means of selection into different areas of the workforce. Hence they tend to treat the concept of the hidden curriculum as if it were the same for all groups of children. Marxists also find the idea of the hidden curriculum to be useful. Unlike the functionalists, however, they suggest that the hidden curriculum works differently for children from different social classes. Since they are skeptical about the claim that schools provide equal opportunity, they have not accepted the assumption that the hidden curriculum is presented in the same way to all children, nor have they assumed that all children receive the curriculum that is presented to them in the same manner.

In one study Jean Anyon draws upon aspects of the Marxist tradition in order to study the workings of the hidden curriculum.[1] She examined the fifth-grade classrooms in five different schools and found significant differences in the way in which conceptions of work, ownership, rules, and decision making were presented through the hidden curriculum. The children in four of the five schools came from different social-class backgrounds. Two of the schools had working-class populations, one a middle-class population, one an upper-middle-class population, and one an "executive elite" population. Anyon found that each of these schools exhibited a different pedagogical style. While the style of teaching differed significantly between schools, it remained quite similar from subject to subject within the same school. Hence, whether the subject matter was arithmetic, language arts, science, or social studies, the hidden curriculum remained the same for children in the working-class school and the hidden curriculum within this school differed from that which was found in each of the other schools. In every case, however, Anyon found that the hidden curriculum presented certain conceptions of work, ownership, rules, and authority. The nature of these conceptions differed from one school to the next, and these differences correlated to social-class background.

In the working-class school, for example, Anyon reported that much of the work expected of the children was mechanical and rote. Children were allowed to make few decisions; the teacher "rarely explained why work was assigned, how it connected to other assignments," or what its general significance was.[2] Rules were presented to the children as step-by-step processes that were always to be followed and never circumvented. This held true even if a child suggested a more efficient way to do the task at hand. Anyon illustrates this observation with the following conversation from a math class:

> One of the teachers led the children through a series of steps to make a one-inch grid on the paper without telling them that they were making a one-inch grid, or that it would be used to study scale. She said, "Take your ruler. Put it across the top. Make a mark at every number. Then move your ruler down to the bottom. . . ." At this point a girl said that she had a faster way to do it and the teacher said, "No you don't; you don't even know what I'm making yet. Do it this way, or it's wrong."[3]

The same lock-step method of teaching was apparent in all the other subjects taught in this school. Language arts consisted of teaching the children the mechanics of punctuation. There was a rule for each and every punctuation mark, and breaking the rule was never justifiable. An autobiography was "written by filling in the blanks on a page in response to such questions as 'Where were you born?' and 'What is your favorite animal?' "[4] In this school the teacher attempted to exert total control over the use of time and space in the classroom and to maintain complete authority in the making of decisions. The items in the room were spoken of as the teacher's property, and the students were to handle them as she directed. Classroom control was established by direct orders such as "open your books," "shut up," and so forth.

The affluent, upper-middle-class school presented a marked contrast to the working-class school. Here the hidden curriculum provided a startlingly different conception of rules, authority, and property. In language arts the emphasis was on creative writing. Principles of punctuation were taught, but children learned that the placement of a punctuation mark depends upon the meaning that *they* want to communicate. Correct punctuation was a matter for group discussion. Control of the classroom was carried on through negotiation. Even when a student left the classroom, no pass was required. Students just signed their names on the chalkboard.

Anyon's analysis of these schools is an example of the way in which a Marxist perspective extends the concept of the hidden curriculum to show how it works to reproduce the relations of production. In Anyon's study the working-class students are being taught how to participate in the world of work at the lower end of the production process. They are being taught to follow rules that are not understood, to engage in work that has little meaning for them, and to follow without question the orders issued by an external authority. Students in the upper-middle-class school are being taught how to engage in the world of work at a relatively high level. They are being taught to work independently, to judge for themselves whether a rule meets the larger purpose of the task at hand, to manipulate symbols to their own ends, to exercise internal discipline, and to negotiate with authority on an equal basis. In Anyon's study the middle-class schools and the executive-elite schools presented still different pictures of rules and authority. The first taught students the behaviors and attitudes required to follow accepted form and to find the "right answers," which were located in some authoritative text. In the executive-elite school the children were taught to manage situations in which they were expected to be in charge.[5]

Anyon's study is quite limited in its scope. It is, after all, restricted to the fifth-grade classrooms of a few, somewhat rare, homogeneous schools. However, its basic empirical findings are supported by other studies, some of which are outside of the neo-Marxist tradition. For example, Ray McDermott (whose work we will look at more closely in the next part of this book), in a microanalysis of classroom behavior, has found that students from the high reading group interrupt the teacher quite frequently when she is working with students from the lower reading groups. However, students from the lower groups are much less likely to cross over into the space occupied by the high reading group to interrupt the teacher. McDermott does not explicitly relate these and similar findings to the socioeconomic class of the children, and hence his study falls outside of the Marxist tradition. However, it does support the view that the hidden curriculum works differently for different types of students.[6] Similarly, Ray Rist, drawing on quite a different tradition, has found that teachers tend to classify students very early in their school life on the basis of nonacademic attributes, such as neatness of dress, and then to treat the students according to these classifications. Teachers will tend to interact much more frequently with those students who come to school well groomed and will give much more attention to their academic work.[7] Like McDermott, Rist does not suggest that reproducing the relations of production explains this classification. His study also falls outside the Marxist tradition. However, Anyon clearly does want to say that the need to reproduce the relations of production in a capitalist society is the cause of the different forms of the hidden curriculum. But, other than showing that there is a correlation between the class status of the parents and the hidden curriculum of the school, the causal connection is not established. A correlation is not necessarily a causal connection. Nevertheless, Anyon's study provides some interesting implications for reassessing the functionalist view of schooling. You might want to consider the case of "Class Bias" in chapter 8 to explore some of these issues further.

A Theory of Cultural Reproduction

Perhaps the most elaborate theoretical work on the issue of educational reproduction comes from two French scholars, Pierre Bourdieu and Jean-Claude Passeron.[8] Drawing partially on the Marxist tradition, they argue that schooling produces certain deep-seated ways of understanding and perceiving that allow subordinate groups to be reproduced and the dominant class to maintain its status without resorting to physical repression or coercion. In other words, what they call "symbolic violence" substitutes for physical violence. Symbolic violence is the imposition of the meaning system of one group onto that of another. They call the deep-seated ways of perceiving and understanding that develop in this process the "habitus." It is the elements of perception, understanding, and style that are passed on from one generation to the next, binding the members of a cultural group together and separating them from the members of other cultural groups. While the habitus serves to separate group from group, it also serves to provide legitimacy to the symbols of the dominant culture. The school is the primary agency for establishing this legitimacy, and it does so by developing in the members of the subordinate culture a distant respect for the unapproachable objects and symbols of the dominant culture ordinarily found in such institutions as museums, concert halls, and "the classics." Because the school presents itself as an apolitical and neutral forum, Bourdieu and Passeron believe that those in the subordinate cultures come to accept the claim to cultural superiority that is made for the symbols of the dominant culture. Members of the subordinate groups learn to blame themselves for their "cultural insensitivity." The school reproduces a certain outlook that is typical of one's class background. This outlook involves both the way in which people perceive the symbols and meaning of the dominant culture and the way in which they perceive their own placement in the social structure. Bourdieu and Passeron argue that the perception of schooling as a neutral, apolitical selection mechanism conceals the ever-present bias in selection and provides the appearance of objectivity and fairness.

Although Bourdieu and his collaborators have compiled some sophisticated empirical evidence to support their views, many of their most convincing arguments are based on commonsense observations. For example, many traditional supporters of schools defend the claim that the school is a fair and reasonable selection mechanism by pointing to the objective tests that are used to move students from one level to the next. However, as Bourdieu and Passeron point out, the vast majority of youngsters do not lose out in a formal competition that results in their rejection from prestigious institutes of learning. Rather, well before the competition begins most students calculate their chances of success from the standpoint of their social-class position and make a decision not to enter the competition at all. Moreover, those who do compete and who do so more or less successfully are still marked by the cultural style they bring with them to their studies.

While Bourdieu and Passeron's study provides some fascinating insights about the process of reproduction, it also has a number of problems. In the first place, little in their work suggests that any significant differences of kind are to be found among the various cultural subgroups they discuss. Rather, it appears that all differences are differences of degree and depend upon how distant a group is from the symbolic forms of the dominant culture. Their own analysis provides us with some understanding of the way in which the dominant cultural forms are appropriated with varying success by different cultural subgroups. It does not, however, provide us with an understanding of the nature of these subgroups themselves.

For example, some of Bourdieu's work involves a statistical analysis of the frequency with which members of different groups utilize certain kinds of cultural institutions, such as museums, concert halls, theaters, and so forth. One of the points of this analysis is to show that the forms of higher culture are mainly utilized by those who have acquired the code to decipher these cultural presentations.[9] The point is not primarily that this code is or is not learned in school. Indeed, the family may well be the more effective agent for teaching (or not teaching) the code through which the symbols of the dominant culture are deciphered. The more important point is that the schools teach children to evaluate their own standing in relation to their ability to decipher this kind of cultural material. Yet without a more specific understanding of the subgroups being considered, it is difficult to know whether or not this is true, and if it is true, then in what sense and to what degree.

Through Bourdieu's work, and through commonsense observation, we know that the forms of high culture are utilized more frequently by prestigious groups than by others. Yet we do not really know what this utilization means. Is there a true appreciation of the cultural form, or is concert-going, for example, simply a way of meeting a social expectation? Bourdieu assumes that going to the theater or to a concert implies that one has acquired the code to appreciate what is going on, an assumption that is probably true for some and not for others. The same problem seems to hold for the treatment of the lower-status groups. Bourdieu simply assumes that infrequent utilization of certain cultural forms means that the code for appreciating these cultural presentations has not been made available to members from these groups. However, we do not know what the failure to attend certain kinds of cultural events means to members of these groups. Moreover, we know very little about the meaning of their presence at the events they do attend. That is, we know very little, given Bourdieu's treatment, about the nature of the culture of these subgroups. Bourdieu simply assumes that the code for deciphering the materials of the dominant culture has not been made available to members of these groups. He does not consider the possibility that the code may have been presented to them, but that for some reasons of their own they have decided to resist learning it.

When it comes to the issue of reproduction and resistance, this oversight is important. If a subculture is looked upon as simply a pale reflection of the dominant culture, with little integrity of its own, then the prospects for any kind of resistance to domination or oppression would seem to be blunted from the start. Indeed, one of the most serious problems with Bourdieu's theoretical framework is that it provides little reason and few tools for analyzing the perspectives of different cultural subgroups. Given this failing, he provides no reason to believe that the form of cultural domination he describes can be broken in any significant way.[10]

Student Subculture and the Working Class

The actual process of reproducing and legitimizing the relations of production seems to be significantly more complex than the picture drawn by the Marxist researchers considered thus far. The British researcher Paul Willis, however, provides a much more thorough and detailed picture of the contours of a student culture in its interaction with the formal structure of the school. This picture suggests that there is a much more active, even critical, involvement on the part of working-class youngsters in determining their own fate. Willis objects to those studies, such as that by Bourdieu and Passeron, that insist upon viewing working-class children as simply reacting in a passive, unconscious way to the forces around them as they are propelled to take up their "inevitable" place in the world of work. As Willis puts it, "The difficult thing to explain about how working-class kids get working-class jobs is why they let themselves."[11] The way the question is put suggests that there is some element of choice involved for children from this cultural group.

The focus of Willis's ethnographic study, which is set in England, is twelve working-class, secondary-school boys called "the lads," who attend a nonselective secondary school that Willis calls "Hammertown Boys." The lads are a closely knit group of friends who form their own subculture within the school. They define themselves in opposition to the formal school structure and to other students, whom they call the "ear'oles" and whom they see as dutiful conformists to the school's policy. Willis's study began in the second term of the next to last year in school and followed the lads through six months of their working life after graduation. His study is worth describing here in some detail because it represents the most complete attempt that we have to understand the way in which class consciousness is formed in the context of schooling.

Willis describes how the informal culture of the lads and the formal structure of the school stand in opposition to one another. They are in a constant contest over power and control. The school stands as the well-organized, formal institution. It has a defined structure, a clear hierarchy, and an elaborate set of rules.[12] The lads are nonconformists and troublemakers. Yet the effect of this resistance, as Willis describes it, is that the lads will wind up as unskilled or semiskilled workers who are well prepared to perform unpleasant, routine, heavy manual labor. In essence, Willis's study shows the complex process by which labor power of a certain kind is reproduced and reproduces itself.

The school, of course, does not have enough physical resources to maintain order by its punitive power alone. It must rely a good deal on its moral authority and on the acceptance of that authority by the majority of students. As Willis puts it, "The teacher's authority must be won and maintained on moral, not on coercive grounds. There must be consent from the taught."[13] This moral authority is cemented for most students when they accept the basic exchange that the teachers offer them in various ways. The bargain is struck along the following lines. If the students give the teachers respect, then the teachers will give meaningful knowledge in return, which will lead to a marketable credential, which will then provide access to a rewarding job. While most students are willing to accept this bargain, the lads are not. They reject the moral authority upon which the formal structure of the school depends, a rejection that rests upon a reasonable calculation of their own chances for success and upon a realistic appraisal of the requirements demanded by the type of work that is likely to be available to them. However, Willis observes that the process of rejection involves the development by the lads of their own cultural framework and a creative reinterpretation of the messages presented by the school.

While the lads' resistance is counterproductive in the long run, it is nevertheless effective for them in the short run. By establishing their oppositional culture in the school, they are well prepared for life on the shop floor. Indeed, it is their rejection and reinterpretation of the school message that allows them to function in the work world at a level of comfort that is not available to the ear'oles. Given their horizons, there is no meaningful work. Work does not exist to establish an identity or to provide them with a special and separate status or to develop their self-concept, as middle-class culture tries to tell them. Rather, work exists to provide wages that then allow them the freedom outside of work to do what they wish. The chances are strong that the lads will end up with precisely the kinds of dead-end jobs that they envisage. However, their own perceptions add an additional force to that probability.

Having rejected the last part of the teachers' bargain, everything else quickly falls into place. If there are no meaningful jobs, then there is no useful credential. And if the credential is supposed to signal the possession of some kind of important knowledge, then it is a lie. The knowledge provided in the school, theoretical understanding of such areas as math and science, has no relevance on the shop floor where practical know-how is all important. To the lads, theoretical knowledge is associated with that which is feminine, while practical know-how is seen as truly masculine knowledge. Having rejected the knowledge offered by the school, it is a natural step for the lads to see the respect that is demanded by the teachers as an illegitimate imposition, an unwarranted and oppressive feature of the formal school culture.

The ironic fact is that the lads' school culture has many similarities with the work that most of them will be performing on the shop floor. The shop, much like the school subculture, has a strongly masculine atmosphere, where both sexism and racism are powerful components. In the shop the men value the practical and degrade the theoretical. This devaluing of mental work provides license for the men on the shop floor to continue to resist the authority of the boss, much in the same way that it gave the lads license to resist the authority of the teacher. Mental labor is effeminate; it is something to be seen through and exposed, not something to be respected and followed.

Thus the lads' culture prepares them well for the experience that they will find in the shop. However, one must ask: Just how does this preparation serve the owners of the shop? To answer this question, we need only recall the nature of the work that is performed in the shop and the limited prospects that it provides for escape or upward mobility. The lads come not only prepared for the worst, but prepared to accept it with bravado. What more could a boss ask for? Unlike the ear'oles, the lads do not expect to find their identity in their work. They do not expect to be promoted for superior performance, and unlike the ear'oles, they are not disappointed and discouraged when such rewards are not forthcoming.

In the short run the lads' subculture prepares them very well for the world that they find in the shop. Of course, their own perspective and antagonistic framework also blocks them from pursuing any other alternative and thus from finding a better life. The ideals of equal opportunity and upward mobility are a reflection of the liberal, functional, individualistic logic, a logic that both Willis and the lads, in different ways, reject. Capitalism does allow some individuals to escape their class background and move into higher and more rewarding jobs. The high salaries paid to people in professional sports is a good, but extreme, example. To execute such an escape it is also helpful to believe that it is possible. Yet this is an alternative that only a few individuals can take advantage of. Belief in the system may be a prerequisite for individual success, but it is not a guarantee, and for most people it is not sufficient. The lads perceive that this belief is appropriate only from the point of view of an individualistic logic. From the point of view of the group, it provides no alternatives at all. From this perspective, the lads' decision to establish meaning for their lives outside of the formal work and school situation makes sense. It is, in Willis's terms, a real *penetration* into the nature and the logic of the capitalist system.

Yet the strategy that pays off in the short run is productive neither for the individual nor the group in the long run. Work provides the lads with the exhilaration that comes with a sudden jump in income, as Willis points out. It provides them with direct contact with the world of masculine work, a major theme of their school counterculture. In the long run, however, it serves the needs neither of the individual nor of the class, as the lads will find themselves day after day performing the same routine jobs in the same meaningless way without a really clear idea of the forces that oppress them or of the alternative courses of action that might be taken.

While one cannot be optimistic about the prospects for the lads, Willis believes that this kind of close cultural analysis is essential if any form of collective liberation is to be facilitated. The lads are indeed limited by their own racism and sexism. They are also limited by their bravado acceptance of hard, routine, manual labor. Yet, to Willis's eye, a close study of the cultures of the working class is able to reveal the potential points of creative resistance, points that conceivably could be used to force progressive and collective change.

The lads appear as tragic characters. How would a functionalist attempt to explain to them the harm they are doing to themselves? How could the school's structure be justified? Criticized? How would a Marxist explain the lads' situation to them? What, if any, prescription could a Marxist give to the lads or to a teacher in order to help develop a truly critical consciousness? After answering these questions, you might want to consider the "Social Studies" case in chapter 8 and the question, Does hard work in school pay off?

Puzzles, Problems, and Prospects

Marxists provide a sharp and critical view of functionalism, viewing it as an essentially ideological position that uses science to justify the institutions of modern society. Yet they are unclear about which aspects of this criticism are the most serious. Is the problem that functionalism is essentially ideological while Marxism is not? Or that functionalism is an ideology that serves to justify the institutions of modern society, whereas Marxism, which is also an ideology, serves to criticize modern institutions? If the former is the case, then Marxism needs to provide a criterion for separating an ideological from a scientific position. The development of such a criterion has proved elusive for Marxists and non-Marxists alike. If the problem is not one of ideology versus science, but rather the nature and purpose of the ideology presented by functionalism, then Marxism needs to develop a statement that will allow us to evaluate competing ideologies on normative grounds. Marxists have avoided developing such a statement, probably because their position requires that norms be understood in relation to one's class position. However, the failure to develop a normative position tends to move Marxism uncomfortably close to functionalism and the problems associated with it. Take Giddens's criticism of functionalism as an example.

Whereas functionalists will explain a school practice in terms of its adaptive value for society as a whole, Marxists will explain it in terms of the way in which it serves the interests of the capitalist class. Does this mean, however, that the interests of the capitalist class are to be taken as the cause of the practice? If it does mean this, then Giddens's criticism of functionalism holds equally well for Marxism. That is, the Marxist seems to presuppose some system need. In this case, however, the need is not that of the social system as a whole, but of the capitalist class. Yet, Giddens's observation that the "notion of 'need' is falsely applied if it is not acknowledged that system needs presuppose actors' wants"[14] holds equally well here. Class needs also presuppose actors' wants.

There are other problems with the claim that the structure of schooling can be causally explained by the interests of capitalism. Consider the fact that the United States is not the only capitalist society in the world. Yet there are significant differences between the schools of the United States and those of other countries with similar economies, such as Japan, France, England, or Taiwan. Indeed, in some countries with a more established (although not dominant) socialist tradition, such as England and France, the schools appear to be more hierarchical than in the United States, which has a limited socialist tradition. Willis's study, after all, was of children from the English working class. Moreover, some specific aspects of schooling, such as the timing and length of the school summer vacation in the United States, have little to do with capitalism itself. This particular practice is more adequately explained as a remnant from a more agricultural society, in which children were needed to work the farm during the summer months. While there are some practices that might be better understood by reference to the interests of capitalism, there are other practices that are more appropriately understood in other ways. The appeal to the interests of capitalism carries a certain moral force because it is implicitly set off against another oppositional and more justifiable interest—the humane education of the child. Yet Marxists have not developed their ideas about this oppositional interest into a positive statement about the preferred direction of education and pedagogy.

Willis's study is somewhat of an exception to the above remarks. While it does not offer much guidance for the development of a positive pedagogy, it does provide an understanding of the way in which the interest of one class—the capitalists—is mediated through the wants of members of another class—the lads' working-class culture—to produce part of a causal chain. The effect of this chain for the lads is, of course, to reproduce the values, attitudes, and behavior required to work at the lower end of the production process.

With other forms of Marxism, Willis's study stands in opposition to the functionalist point of view. It challenges the belief that schools provide a universal and unbiased set of standards by which talent can be identified, trained, and rewarded. It reminds us that schools are as much involved in developing labor power for the lower end of the industrial hierarchy as in developing the "brain power" for the upper end.

While Willis's study shares this much with traditional forms of Marxism, it also stands in opposition to much that is associated with Marxist thought. Instead of focusing on universal laws of development, as both functionalists and orthodox Marxists have done, Willis accepts a more open and unpredictable view of change. Instead of viewing the economic structure as the key to consciousness, his study allows us to understand how consciousness may work to preserve an oppressive economic structure for some segment of the working class. Rather than focusing exclusively upon the larger economic and political structures as the unit of analysis, Willis focuses on the meaning system and wants of the local subculture. In this way his work comes close to developing a causal explanation of the reproduction of labor that takes into account individual wants.

Clearly Willis's study is limited. Its focus is on the working class in England. Indeed, it is really on a very small subset of males within that working class, and it is not clear just how much we might generalize from his study. Moreover, while Willis's study provides a good deal of insight into the meaning system of the lads and the way in which that system mediates the messages that are sent by the school, it does not provide us with an understanding of how we or they might be able to gain access to other more inclusive systems of meaning and thus break the cycle of reproduction.

Foucault and the Post Modern Move Beyond Marxism

The studies by scholars like Bourdieu and Willis suggest that even before the fall of the Soviet Union, Marxism had moved away from the strictly mechanical emphasis on economic determinism. In their work the focus of attention is on the way in which meaning that is reproduced within certain groups serves to reinforce class position and hierarchy.

The focus on meaning and its reproduction can also be seen in the work of the non-Marxist, Michael Foucault. Foucault may be classified as a conflict theorist, but this does not really do justice to the complexity of his ideas. His work explores the discursive social practices that enter into the formation of human subjects, the ways in which external forces of control are internalized. Or, to separate him from traditional conflict theorists, he believes that we learn to conform to the norms of external surveillance and hence to control ourselves. The social meanings of normalcy, for example, force us to try to conform to dominant views of what is socially acceptable behavior.

While Foucault was not an educational theorist, his ideas throw much light on the influence of the school as it defines sexuality, pleasure, and legitimate activity in ways that students will come to accept as normal. He showed that people may be oppressed and dominated through standard ways of talking that serve to "normalize" certain practices and to "marginalize" others. Think, for example, of the school yard jokes people tell about homosexuals, or that boys learn to tell about girls or girls about boys, as examples of the way norms of sexuality and gender are established, with some people placed at the center of society while others are placed, or place themselves, at the margins. When a practice is normalized, as for example in the acceptability of sexual union between heterosexual partners or in the way in which we accept the privilege associated with being born white, it is uncritically accepted as the standard, or as the right way to be. And when a practice is marginalized, as for example in homosexual unions or in the behavior and conditions associated with some "minority" populations, it is seen as deviant or threatening. Foucault challenges not just the deprivation that minority groups may suffer, or the privilege that majority groups may enjoy. He challenges the entire system of identity that such classification both promotes and provides. He does this by showing how many of our basic categories of thinking, the categories that we use to organize our world, are socially constructed. This means that we did not always divide up the world in precisely the way we do now, and that if we reach back in time, we will find that people often thought in radically different terms than we do. Hence, according to Halperin,[15] a follower of Foucault, people did not always think in terms of homosexuality and heterosexuality. He notes that the term *homosexuality* was introduced into the *Oxford English Dictionary* in 1892 and that there are societies where such distinctions are not made. Rather, "homosexuality" and "heterosexuality," according to Halperin, are tied to a deeper cultural fiction of "sexuality."

Sexuality is to be distinguished from biological differences between men and women. It provides a way to identify individuals according to a set of behaviors that are established as "normal" in a society. In other words, it is a category that belongs to ideology rather than to biology. And, as each of us comes to think of ourselves sexually as a "man" or a "woman," we also begin to judge our own behavior in terms of the "standards" that have been constructed for a person of our gender. In this way our own subjectivity is established, and it is used to establish internal controls that correspond to external practices. Schools are of course one of the most important sites for building an individual's subjectivity and identity. Teachers often expect boys to be assertive, stoical, and competitive and girls to be passive, emotional, and noncompetitive and they arrange their classrooms in ways that reinforce these expectations. To see how prominent a role sexual identity plays in our lives, notice your response when you hear a vocalist whose sex is not immediately identifiable. Is your attention to the song diverted until you figure out the sex of the singer? Do you evaluate the voice differently if you think it is a man but find out it is a woman? Or, notice your puzzlement regarding a person whose sex you cannot immediately identify and the way in which your mind insists on identifying the *real sex of the person*. Foucault would see these as signs of the way in which we have learned to accept certain categories as normal and to insist that everyone must fit in one or another of those categories.

Unlike Marxists, Foucault does not concentrate on problems of oppression where one class appropriates the labor of another. He focuses rather on problems of domination where people are disciplined "to believe themselves to be persons having a certain nature."[16] And the object of such domination is to confine and constrict our identities by shaving and shaping desires and perceptions—the way we feel and see. Connolly expresses this well:

> The human animal is essentially incomplete without social form; and a common language, institutional setting, set of traditions, and political forum for enunciating public purposes are indispensable to the acquisition of an identity and the commonalties essential to life. But every form of social completion and enablement also contains subjugations and cruelties within it.[17]

Marxists also recognize the problems involved in domination, but they seem to believe that given certain revolutionary economic changes, these problems will be resolved. Foucault is not so optimistic about an ultimate and total liberation. As long as social discourse continues and as long as social institutions function, domination will likely occur. The problem then is to find ways to interrupt and to interrogate standard practices and socially constructed meanings. It is to find local sites of resistance.

At first glance, some of Foucault's work, such as the introduction to a hermaphrodite's diary[18] or commentary on the case of a nineteenth-century mass murderer,[19] has a voyeuristic quality about it. However, the object of these studies is not to sensationalize but to explore the medical discourse that developed to control people who are clearly at the margins of society. These studies fit into a larger body of theoretical studies that analyze the development of modern institutions, such as asylums, clinics, and jails, and the practices of psychological and sexual counseling.

The impetus behind these studies is Foucault's belief that the modern world is marked by a ubiquitous discourse that serves to "normalize" people and to subordinate them to certain regimes of knowledge and power. It is likely that Foucault's status as a gay man sensitized him to the various ways in which society forces people to assume that certain ways of doing and thinking are normal, and marginalizes all of those who do and think otherwise. It is likely, too, that his turn away from Marxism, influenced as it was by large political events, was equally influenced by those micro events that occur in the living room, across a neighbor's fence, or in a school classroom. Foucault's work, whether on the theoretical level,[20] or on the historical,[21] or on marginalized individuals, presents a mirror of our own discourse, of the ways it internalizes power relations, marginalizes otherness, and conceals alternative identity formations.[22]

Foucault's work draws much of its appeal from his steadfast refusal to provide any blueprint for the development of subjects, although he clearly would prefer that people become more reflective about taken-for-granted aspects of identity. This refusal is consistent with his concern that we find ways to interrupt and interrogate various modes of domination and control. If he were then to turn around and advance one identity over others, he would be in danger of lending his authority to a new orthodoxy and hence to a new form of domination and control. This concern to develop a heightened understanding of taken-for-granted aspects of our identity while refusing to tell us what, if any, new forms identity might take, has important implications for education. It has been especially important for people working to revise the sex education curriculum and to enable schools to end the silences that gay or sexually active students find in the classroom and to address their concerns as well as the concerns of those parents and community leaders who wish to promote abstinence.[23]

Yet if the refusal to offer a preferred identity is one of Foucault's strengths, it is also a problem. Recall Connolly's words: "The human animal is essentially incomplete without social form; and a common language, institutional setting, set of traditions, and political forum for enunciating public purposes are indispensable to the acquisition of an identity and the commonalties essential to life." Although Foucault (and Connolly) reminds us that if we fully identify with such forms we risk shaving our identity too close to the skin, this does not eliminate the fact that we always choose among less than perfect possibilities. Foucault serves as a reminder of this choice, but provides little guidance in helping us to understand how to make it.

Foucault's influence on contemporary social movements has been considerable. He has, among other things, helped us to see how groups that do not fit neatly into Marxists' classification could still suffer from relationships of domination. Given the corruption of Marxist political regimes and the change in forms of government in Eastern Europe and the former Soviet Union, it is important to remember that there is more to domination than class oppression or governmental regimentation. In providing this insight he has also developed some of the tools that have enabled newer movements to liberate themselves from an over reliance on Marxists concepts and understandings. This has been especially important given the dramatic changes in the international political climate since the fall of the Soviet Union, and the increasing prominence of feminist theory and practice.

Feminism as a Form of Conflict Theory

The relationship between feminism and Marxism has not always been an easy one. On the one hand, Marxists have gone further than most in recognizing the subordinate position of women. On the other hand, Marxists have tended to explain this position in terms of the means of production and the class division of labor. The problem is that not all women are members of the working class and so it is hard, from a Marxist point of view, to explain why a movement should be devoted to liberating all women. By observing that oppression and domination occur beyond class formations, Foucault, among others, has helped address that problem.

In its most general form feminism is a political, social, intellectual, and artistic movement that strives, in Jaggar's terms, to eliminate the subordination of women.[24] Feminists differ from Marxists, however, in at least two important respects. First, they hold that there is an additional dimension to oppression and domination that goes beyond social class, and this is sexual oppression. Indeed, by focusing exclusively on the element on social class Marxists have, according to this view, under-emphasized the extent to which women from all social classes are dominated by men. Hence while many feminists agree with Marxists that oppression is a basic element of social life, they disagree that a focus on class alone is sufficient. If we want to explain and address oppression, we must go beyond the class division of labor and look as well to the sexual division.

Marxists often overlooked the sexual division of labor, sometimes assuming that it had a more solid foundation in the nature of things, and Marx, although recognizing its corruption by capitalism, used the ideal of the family as a metaphor for a more perfect society. However, feminists hold that there is little reason to exclude the family from scrutiny and that oppressive relations are as likely to occur within the family as within the work place. Indeed, the problems associated with the sexual division of labor are even more pervasive than those associated with class. Unlike the class division of labor, the sexual division occurs not only within the job site but at home as well, and feminists have addressed both of these.

Within the work place sexual domination occurs in a number of different ways. The reluctance to hire or promote a woman, even when she may be the most qualified person for a position, is the most obvious example. Companies have historically favored men for a number of reasons. They may assume that a woman applicant may have more responsibilities inside of the home, caring for children or for elderly parents, and thus conclude that her commitment to the company will be compromised. Or, they may assume that an entire family depends on a man's income whereas a woman's is supplemental. Or, because the officers of companies are usually men, they may find that they are just more comfortable working around other men. Whatever the reason may be, the effect has been to block qualified women out of positions.

The tendency to favor men over women has had a strong impact on education. Since women were not expected to occupy important positions outside of the home, the educational expectations for girls have been different from those for boys. For example, many fewer girls have taken advanced mathematics and science courses, and girls tend to ask fewer questions than boys and are generally less assertive in the classroom. This behavior reinforces sexist assumptions that girls are less able to perform at the higher levels of math and science. And these assumptions are likely to guide not only the work of teachers and administrators, but the self-understanding and the desires of girls themselves. Thus girls may under-estimate their own ability or reject a natural inclination for science or math in order not to appear too competitive or to outdo the boys.

In the end, all of these factors, the different opportunities for men and women at work, the different curricula for boys and girls in school, the sexist assumptions by teachers and administrators about the abilities of boys and girls and the lower academic self-esteem and ambition of girls reinforce one another. To change one may require a change in them all.

Yet what might it mean to change one of these factors. Let us begin with the world of work. Many feminists believe that it is not sufficient to simply establish fair procedures of selection so that qualified women will be able to compete on an equal basis with qualified men. In addition it is important to recognize that work roles have been structured by men to fit the work patterns of men. As Mackinnon notes: most positions, however gender neutral the requirements may be, are not set up for a person who is the primary caretaker of a young child.[25] Incidentally, her observation marks one of the flaws in the functionalist position. A set of interrelated practices may be highly functional, but they may still be wrong from an ethical point of view.

Thus the problems involved in fair selection of men and women candidates are not restricted to the work place, but extend into deeply held cultural practices and beliefs about home life, the raising of children, and the independence of women. These beliefs and their impact especially on poor women is captured by Nancy Fraser,[26] who observes that public aid holds discriminatory assumptions about the needs of men and women and that these assumptions translate into very different need-delivery systems. For most men aid comes in the form of unemployment insurance. This aid involves cash payments and allows the recipient to use the money in whatever manner he chooses. Thus public aid to men assume that the recipient has rights and that the state cannot dictate how that aid is spent. The situation for many women is considerably different. Here most aid has historically come in the form of Aid to Dependent Children and various other defined programs such as food stamps. This kind of aid is highly restrictive and defines not only what a woman may and may not do with the aid, but also how she may or may not behave. In many cases, for example, when women received child support or public housing, they were forbidden to have men living with them.

Yet it is not just poor women who are affected by the way in which society appropriates the public and the private realm according to the sexual division of labor. Women from all strata of society have been limited in their opportunities because they have been defined in their totality by but one feature of their being— their ability to biologically produce children. Many feminists allow that there are significant differences between men and women that society needs to take into account in structuring work and education. However, these differences should not be used to wall off women from the engagement with meaningful lives outside of the home or to restrict men from enhancing their roles in child rearing and home making. Moreover, most differences between men and women that are taken to define the two sexes are not essential differences but rather represent statistical averages, averages that are often heavily influenced by social tradition and practices. For example, while on average women may be more caring and less assertive than men, yet there are many men who are quite caring and many women who are quite assertive. Thus it is important to be careful in assigning a certain characteristic to a given sex.

Having said this, however, many feminists correctly note that one of the effects of a sexist society is the devaluation of the special insights and virtues that women often bring to a situation. Hence, for example, educational scholars like Carol Gilligan[27] and Nel Noddings[28] have argued that too much attention has been paid to the virtue of justice and too little to the virtue of care. Gilligan has shown how much of the research on moral education and moral development has focused on a predominantly male occupation with issues of justice, and has simply failed to understand the importance that girls place on caring for and maintaining relationships. Until recently this difference has either been mistaken by male behavioral scientists to suggest that girls tended towards a slower stage of moral development than boys, or by a patriarchal society to define girls in terms of marriage, home making, and motherhood.

Once these difference are understood within the context of a feminism that no longer accepts traditional patriarchal assignments as natural, we can intervene in the educational process so that schools are not used to relegate women and men to predefined social roles. Girls can be encouraged to take higher level math and science and to use their ability to nurture one another to develop cooperative learning environments in which everyone can excel, and boys can learn to cherish the intellectual insights of their classmates without thinking that they are being upstaged.

Feminism may be seen as a form of conflict theory, and to some extent it is. However, feminism may also be consistent with certain forms of functionalism. For example, functionalists could hold that certain practices related to the sexual division of labor might once have been appropriate because of limited technology, the brutalizing nature of much industrial labor, primitive birth control techniques, etc. However, they could also agree with feminists that many of these practices are no longer appropriate given the changes in scientific and technical knowledge. Whether we accept a conflict model, a functionalism model, or something else, feminism redirects our attention and asks that we look beyond the structure of work or the division of labor and that we attend as well to the pervasive social meanings and assumptions that are called forth by different practices. In the next chapter we turn to the question of meaning and explore how we understand something and what is entailed in rendering an interpretation.

Part IV

INTERPRETATION AND THE SOCIAL FUNCTION OF SCHOOLING

Chapter 6

The Interpretivist
Point of View

In the preceding chapters you have seen two radically different views of the role of schools in contemporary society. The functionalist argues that schools are an important institution in facilitating the movement toward technological development, material well-being, and democracy. The Marxist views schooling as a major instrument for maintaining and legitimating the domination of one group over another. At this point, you may be expecting us to reconcile these different viewpoints or to provide a third, and more acceptable, position. Unfortunately, since we disagree ourselves about which of these two interpretations best reflects the relation of school to society, we must disappoint that expectation.

Having heard our confession, you may now be saying to yourself, "Well, then, if the authors can't agree about which viewpoint is the more appropriate one, then answers to questions about the role of schools in society must be just a matter of interpretation." If this is your response, we would generally agree with it. However, we would question the appropriateness of the word *just*, for it seems to minimize the importance of the process of interpretation. After all, some interpretations do fit the facts of a specific situation better than others do.

In this chapter, we will consider interpretivism, a very different point of view on the nature of social research and the relation of schools to society. Unlike the functionalist or Marxist, the interpretivist offers no global political argument about the role schools play in society. The interpretivist believes that there are many different roles that schools play in differing contexts. Interpretivism has a *local* rather than a *global* orientation. Interpretivists are more concerned with the culture-bound frameworks of particular schools and the ways individuals understand and act in specific social contexts than with finding general laws or all-encompassing explanations. They view schools as places where groups and individuals interact through local, mutually understood "rules of the game." Therefore, they see their main task as researchers to be that of describing what is going on in particular instances of schooling. This requires an interpretation of the ways people think and act in schools.

The study of *The Good High School*[1] by Sara Lawrence Lightfoot is a good example of interpretivist research. She gives her work the apt subtitle *Portraits of Character and Culture*. She sought to find out what made five quite different schools, in different parts of the country, "good schools." She engaged in in-depth observation of the daily lives of students, teachers, and administrators at the schools, trying to draw a "portrait" of each school that captured the essential features that made each school special in its own way. Just as the good people we all know do not look or act alike, Lightfoot found that each school had its special mix of good characteristics that worked together to make each school uniquely good in its own way. Each also had its "warts" and problems, of course, just as people do; but the overall impression Lightfoot sought to document and the portraits she sought to draw with her words were portraits that captured the essence of "goodness" in each school.

Of course, different artists might draw different portraits of the same person or school. There is no such thing as the correct or true portrait of someone or some school. In this way, interpretivist research differs markedly from functionalist and Marxist research because it does not act on some universal, politically salient theory of explanation nor seek the one true description of social reality. Descriptions for the interpretivist are interpretations.

Perhaps you responded to our confession that we cannot agree about which view best fits the facts in a different way, by saying to yourself, "One or the other (or some third view) must be a true description of what schooling is and does." If you responded in this way, you may have revealed something important that you share with both functionalism and orthodox Marxism. We can begin our discussion of interpretation by looking at the common ground. That is, we can look at the assumption that there is but one true description of the relation of school to society. We can then contrast this assumption with the interpretivist point of view.

Recall that both functionalists and orthodox Marxists believe that, like the physical and natural universe, social behavior is governed by discernible laws. Both believe that if we examine social life scientifically, we should be able to discover certain universal generalizations that govern and accurately describe the development of human societies. They disagree, of course, about the implications of these laws. Functionalists argue, for example, that in modern society there is a strong movement away from distributing rewards and positions on the basis of ascribed values and toward distributing them on the basis of achieved values. Orthodox Marxists, on the other hand, produce evidence suggesting that the distribution of rewards and positions can best be explained in terms of class conflict and the different relations that different classes have to the means of production. Both, however, affirm the view that an adequate explanation of social facts must reflect the kind of explanation that is often associated with the natural sciences; it must be a universally true description of social reality based on objective evidence.

For this reason both functionalists and orthodox Marxists would be leery of the view that we are about to present. They would argue together that to reduce the role of lawful explanation and to elevate the importance of interpretation is to imply that there is not a standard for judging whether an explanation is or is not verifiable. Both Marxists and functionalists would argue that there is such a standard. It is to be found in the model for substantiating theories, laws, and hypotheses provided by the natural sciences. It is based on offering strong evidence for one theory or claim without finding counterevidence that would support a contrary theory or claim. To say that a particular theoretical explanation is just an interpretation may be taken to imply that it does not meet this standard. Ironically, while both functionalists and orthodox Marxists accept such a standard, each denies that the other has met it. Both offer evidence to support their views, but they also provide strong counterevidence against each other's view. While each sees its own view as scientific, it sees the other view as ideological, as politically motivated interpretation.

There are a number of different strategies that might be taken to address the shortcomings of these competing theories. One could argue that even though functionalism and orthodox Marxism fail to meet fully the standards set down for an acceptable scientific explanation, we should not give up the quest for such an understanding of social life. That an adequate scientific explanation with conclusive evidence for it has not yet been provided does not mean that one cannot be developed in the future. One also could argue, however, that any proposed explanation of social life will inevitably fall short of a true scientific explanation because it always must be based on some interpretation and hence be a subjective point of view. This is tantamount to denying that there is any possibility for the development of an objective social science.

Rather than trying to judge the correctness of functionalist and Marxist explanations or determine whether social science is possible, one could reject the basic assumption shared by both—the assumption that the natural sciences as they are commonly understood provide an appropriate model for the understanding of social life. Such a rejection would not imply that a true understanding of human life is impossible. It would mean only that it needs to be sought on different grounds. In modern social sciences, many scholars are trying to develop methodologies to investigate and understand the social world that do not merely imitate the methodology of the natural sciences. It is this movement and its implications for understanding the social function of education that we will explore in this chapter under the general category of the "interpretive point of view." It is this point of view that underwrites the current movement in educational research that has been called qualitative, interpretivist, or constructivist research.

An Argument for the Interpretivist Point of View

One argument against the view that social research should be modeled after research in the natural sciences has been advanced by the British philosopher Peter Winch. Winch has taken a close, critical look at arguments claiming that social behavior must be understood in the same way as natural scientists understand the behavior of physical events. In doing so he rejects the idea that social science can advance by discovering universal regularities through the observation of the "raw behavior" of people in yet-to-be interpreted social events.

Winch argues his case for the importance of interpretation by observing that any kind of understanding, including the understanding displayed by natural scientists, involves the ability to determine when it is that events of the same kind are occurring. He begins by questioning what it is that constitutes a regularity, that is, the "constant recurrence of the same kind of event on the same kind of occasion."[2] He then notes that whether two events are the same depends not only upon the events themselves but also upon the rules that a particular community uses to identify sameness or difference.

A few examples will help to illustrate his point. In the United States a marriage can be established by a formal ceremony that culminates with "I thee wed," "I do," or a number of other such verbal expressions. All of these expressions do the same thing—bind two people into the relationship called marriage. However, under different circumstances, a couple might say these same words and not thereby be married. They might, for example, be acting in a play. And in some states, a marriage can be established even when no vows are taken, as, for example, when a couple lives together in a certain way for a set period of time. All of these (except the acting) are the same thing—marriage—but how do we know that? Certainly not by observing the similarity or sameness of each situation. Rather, we know it because we share a certain language and a social world of common understandings.

Or, to take a contrasting example, a particular "raw behavior" may seem to be the same when removed from any social context, but it can carry very different meanings in different social situations. You raise your hand. In one situation you may be greeting a friend; in another, asking for the teacher's recognition; and in still another, voting. By itself the raw behavior of hand raising has no meaning, even though the muscular activity and the bodily movements in each of these cases is quite similar. The meaning is determined by the way the act is interpreted by the hand raiser and by members of his or her community in a specific context. The following passage by anthropologist Clifford Geertz illustrates the complexities that are involved in determining the meaning of a seemingly simple form of behavior.

> Consider . . . two boys rapidly contracting the eyelids of their right eyes. In one this is an involuntary twitch; in the other, a conspiratorial signal to a friend. The two movements are, as movements, identical; from an I-am-a-camera, "phenomenalistic" observation of them alone, one could not tell which was twitch and which was wink, or indeed whether both or either was twitch or wink. Yet the difference, however unphotographable, between a twitch and a wink is vast; as anyone unfortunate enough to have had the first taken for the second knows. The winker is communicating, and indeed communicating in a quite precise and special way: (1) deliberately, (2) to someone in particular, (3) to impart a message, (4) according to socially established code, and (5) without cognizance of the rest of the company. . . . The winker has not done two things, contracted his eyelids and winked, while the twitcher has done only one, contracted his eyelids. Contracting your eyelids on purpose, when there exists a public code in which so doing counts as a conspiratorial signal *is* winking. That's all there is to it: a speck of behavior, a fleck of culture, and —*Voila*—a gesture.[3]

Because culture provides the larger context in which human messages are interpreted, it is quite likely that the same behavior will be interpreted differently from one culture to another. What is taken as a regularity in one cultural context may not be taken that way in another, and this suggests, at least to Winch, that the primary task of social research is not to uncover universal laws of regularities that can be applied to any culture. It is rather to uncover the specific framework that defines the rules and meanings of cultural life for a specific social group.

Rom Harré and Paul Secord carry this view of "social science" even further.[4] They argue that while natural science is presumably correctly based on a materialistic, mechanical, and causal model of explanation, social science cannot be based solely on that model. To do so, they argue, would be to omit from scientific consideration that which is distinctively human and which accounts for much of human behavior—our shared meanings and understandings of the social situations in which we act. Social behavior is role- and rule-following behavior. However, we do not engage in this behavior in some mechanical way, but in a way that requires human agency, interpretation, understanding, and monitoring.

(Think of the two boys winking in Geertz's example.) More important for our consideration is the recognition that this sort of social behavior is impossible unless the actors have learned the rules of the "social games" they might play. Learning the "rules" for marriage or voting and sharing the social meanings of what these things are makes participating in them possible. Parrots saying, "I do," are not getting married, and raising one's hand to get the teacher's attention is not voting. Socialization, for the interpretivist, becomes learning how to be able to interpret and take part in the "games" people and society "play." However, the socialization process does not determine all our actions, nor does it determine the outcome of those games. According to Harré and Secord, the individual still has a degree of freedom to act on his or her own behalf in deciding what games to play and what to do as an individual while playing them. The ability to interpret what is going on is a key skill. It is required by all forms of socialization. Moreover, social scientists also must be able to interpret behavior. They must be able to interpret the way those who are engaged in an action understand it before they can begin to explain it on other terms. We now turn to look more closely at this key activity of interpretation.

The Active Quality of Mind

The activity of interpretation occurs most clearly in situations where there is some kind of ambiguity needing resolution or where there is a clearly identifiable text, such as a poem, a play, or a novel that needs explication. However, acts of interpretation may occur in other situations as well, and even simple perception seems to require some activities that are similar to those performed in more sophisticated interpretive acts. By examining a special example of perception we can learn more about interpretation. Look at figure 1.

The difficulty we have with this picture is that we can see it in two different ways, as a goblet or as two identical heads that are facing one another. (If you have not yet seen it both ways, continue looking at it until it "switches" for you. If you still cannot see it both ways, ask someone else to point out the heads or goblet you are having trouble seeing.) Because we can come to see the picture in these two ways, we realize that it is not a picture of two heads or of a goblet, even though we can see it *as* one or the other. To recognize that it is the *seeing as* that is important is to acknowledge the role of an active mind in interpreting perceptions. The black and white areas do not change on the page. Our interpretation of the figure as a goblet or as two heads changes. We "read" the "evidence" to support different visual "hypotheses." Whether we call this exercise an

FIGURE 1. "Reading" the "Evidence"

interpretation in the strict sense of the word is a matter of debate. However, it does reveal two elements that are essential to any interpretive activity. The first is the active engagement of the mind trying to "read" or "make sense" of something. The second is the movement from one plausible meaning to another.

The Role of Interpretation in Social Science

Now that we have looked at elements of interpretation in perception, we can turn to look at similar processes as they occur in our interpretation of social situations. We will begin with a fanciful example that draws a strong distinction between the two different views of social science that we have discussed. The first view, shared by functionalist and orthodox Marxists, affirms that the goal of social science is to discover regularities through systematic data gathering and quantitative studies. This also was the dominant form of educational research in the twentieth century. The second view affirms that the goal of social science is to understand the meaning system of the society under study through interpretive engagement and explanation. This is the newer view of the qualitative educational researcher.

Begin by imagining that you are a traditional social scientist visiting the United States for the first time. You are here on a research grant to study American culture, and you have been told that the game of baseball is the key to understanding American life. Now your own culture is very different from the one that you are visiting, and you are aware of this difference on a general level, but you have yet to learn about the specific aspects that separate the two cultures. One of these specific differences is that people in the United States share a concept about sports that is not present in your own society. This is the idea of a "spectator sport," a concept that is taken for granted by American sports lovers, but of which you are unaware. It is not just that you are unaware of the fact that Americans share the concept of a spectator sport; more important, you do not realize that there is such a concept to be shared. Your own culture only has competitive games in which everyone who is present is expected to participate, and everyone does what is expected. No one just *watches* a game. A spectator sport is an inconceivable contradiction in your culture.

On your arrival in the United States you ask your host to take you to a baseball game. You want to study it as a scientist. However, not wanting to contaminate your study with preconceptions, you also request that you not be informed about the nature of the game or its rules. You want to study it objectively and reach your own unbiased conclusions. As a traditionally trained social scientist, one who is looking for universal generalizations, you decide to systematize your observations by measuring the frequency with which certain events follow one another. In this way you hope to establish some correlations and reasonable causal generalizations. (This is similar to the educational researcher who tries to establish a causal relationship between variables such as IQ scores, social class background, and school achievement.) As you begin your data gathering, however, certain problems develop. Since you do not share the concept of a "spectator sport," you also lack other related concepts such as "fan" and "rooting." Moreover, since your host has not informed you about the rules of baseball, you do not have an understanding of the concepts that are specific to that game. Concepts such as "strike," "ball," "hit," and "run" are not a part of your own conceptual framework. Without these concepts it is not even clear what events should be considered as important, and thus it is not clear which events to count in your data gathering. Your difficulty is compounded by the fact that you are not even aware that you lack the key concept of "spectator sport," and hence you are not conscious of the fundamental problem in understanding that is present, even though you might realize that you lack a knowledge of the rules of the game being played.

Because you are unaware of the fact that there is a fundamental difference between your understanding of a "sport" and that of the native American, you begin your investigation by assuming that everyone is playing the game. And "everyone" includes those whom the native American would call fans and players alike. Given this unacknowledged deficiency, the events before your eyes appear totally confusing. There is a lot of throwing and catching of a ball on the field. Some players run from one pillow to another; two others, enclosed in a pen, are throwing and catching another ball. Two players are swinging a club—one is standing and the other, kneeling. Others are motioning as if they were trying to hitch a ride or bless the grass. And still others appear to be trying to consume as much beer as they can.

As you watch more closely, certain features of this strange and confusing scene become more clear. You notice that when those who are throwing and catching the ball on the field leave it to take their underground seats, many of those who have been seated above the ground rise to get more beer, and you begin to think that there is some kind of relation between the two events. However, as you begin to measure the relationship between one and the other, the correlation between the two also seems to be related to other events that happen at the same time as the "beer drinking" and the "sitdown." For example, there seems to be a relationship between the number of times the standing club swinger is able to avoid hitting the ball and the times that the sitdown and the beer drinking occur. However, while this correlation is significant, it is not perfect. Sometimes the thrower is able to hit the club with the ball, and yet both sitting down and drinking beer still follow. However, there is a perfect correlation between the three times that the hitchhiker motions for a ride and yells "out" and the sitdown. There is also a high correlation between the hitchhiker's behavior and the increase in beer drinking. Thus, you conclude that while there is no direct correlation between the sitdown and the beer drinking, there is an indirect one. The hitchhiker causes them both.

With your visit about over and a mass of charts and tables in your hand, you begin to tell your host all that you have learned about the American game of baseball. You admit you still have a way to go to be able to explain everything about the game, but you are confident that you are off to a secure and objective start. Your host looks at the impressive statistics you have gathered and politely praises your methodological skills as a scientist. "Unfortunately," he quietly adds at the end of the conversation, "you have learned nothing at all about baseball."

The host's comment is correct, because you have missed the point of the game. Despite all your impressive statistics, you have failed to understand the reasons behind the observed events. You have failed to grasp the intentions and goals of those who were *really* playing the game and those who were *only* watching. Indeed, you have failed to see that there is an important distinction between participants and spectators in this activity. In other words, you have failed to understand the rules for playing the game of baseball and the "rules" for watching it. It is the rules and their shared understanding by the participants that make baseball the game that it is; and there are also unwritten "rules" for being a fan or a spectator at a game. The interpretivist educational researcher would argue that the same is true for understanding the classroom behaviors of students and teachers.

A complete understanding of baseball requires an understanding of the reasons that a player has for a certain action, and it requires an understanding of the rules of the game, and each must be seen in terms of the other. Moreover, if you want to understand either "game"—that is, being a spectator or being a baseball player—you still need to achieve two interrelated sets of understanding. That is, you need to make sense of the intentions and objectives of individuals in terms of the rules of the "game" they are playing, and you must understand the rules of the fan or player "game." By looking more closely at this analogy with "rules of a game," we will begin to understand some of the factors that are involved in interpreting any social activity, whether it be baseball playing and "fanning," or schooling and "studenting" or "teaching."

Before going on, however, we should look at one important type of misunderstanding found in our baseball example. Observing the relationship between the pitcher and the batter, one of the important misconceptions of our visiting social scientist involved the intentions that motivated their actions. In this case the intentions of the pitcher and the batter were confused. Our social scientist assumed that the pitcher was trying to hit the bat with the ball, and that the batter was trying to avoid having the bat hit. A simple analysis of the behavior alone would be unlikely to tell us that there was something wrong with this interpretation. However, it makes all the difference in the world whether one believes that the pitcher is aiming for the bat or the batter is aiming for the ball. In one case baseball is being played, in the other it is not. The observation and correlation of raw behavior by itself will not tell us which is going on. When a child regularly gives wrong answers, is it because he does not know or because he wants attention? Trying to answer correctly is part of the game of classroom activity. Trying to answer incorrectly is not.

Knowing the intentions of the individual players, however, is not sufficient. Suppose, for example, that a person asks another, "Why are you swinging that club?" and is given the answer, "In order to hit the ball." We still do not know what the person is doing unless we also know the context in which the intent to hit the ball is present. Hitting the ball in baseball is not the same as hitting the ball in tennis or ping-pong. The individual's intent to hit the ball only makes sense in the context of the set of shared rules and goals in which doing so provides an opportunity to get on base, and where getting on base sets the stage for a run and so forth. The same is true of studenting. Trying to give the right answer on a quiz show is not the same as trying to do so in a classroom, where getting something right sets the stage for further learning. In other words, the intention behind an individual's behavior receives meaning in the context of a set of shared rules and goals that allows that behavior to be the activity that the individual intends it to be. To hit a ball in a culture where the game of baseball does not exist may be seen *as* something—ping-pong, practicing for the hunt, or displaced aggression—but it will not be baseball.

The complexity of our baseball example will help us get at the complexity of meanings in any social context. For the interpretivist, meaning is not just something in someone's head, nor is it there in the event just to be read off. The interpretivist realizes that people engage in the activities of social life with some *shared understanding* of the reasons for the activity. They know what is allowed and what is expected. Think of going to church or temple, to school, or to a concert. Part of what makes each of these a meaningful activity for you and others is the shared knowledge of what you are all doing together. People need to interpret what is going on so they can participate in activities in ways meaningful to themselves and to others. Otherwise, they would be as lost and confused in their daily social lives as was our imagined scientific observer at the baseball game.

Now we must ask what it is that people share and know that allows them to act and react meaningfully in the social world—and what the social scientist or educational researcher needs to know to be able to understand their behavior. We have seen that knowledge of the *point* of the activity that people are engaged in is essential. The baseball player is trying to win the game; the fan is seeking relaxation and enjoyment. Buyers and sellers of houses are trying to reach a mutually acceptable price, teachers when teaching are trying to get students to learn things, and students when studying are trying to learn.

Knowing the point of an activity is not enough, however. We have to know how to be a recognized participant in the activity, and we need to know what constitutes engaging in the activity. The point of going to college presumably is to get an education. One could try to do that by spending four years reading in the university library, but that would not count as being a matriculated student on most campuses. Or a person could try to win a baseball game by passing out nausea-causing chewing gum to players on the other team, but that is not playing baseball. There are only certain things that count as playing the game—getting a hit, drawing a walk, catching a fly, passing a test, reading a book, going to classes, and so forth. To be college students or baseball players, we have to know what we and others are supposed to do and what rules govern our activities. There are, of course, the formal rules defining and governing play that are written in the rule books and catalogues. But there are also many, many unwritten rules and conventions, "rules" that govern and define being a batter, a coach, a freshman, and so forth—what constitutes good team work, sportsmanship, and studiousness. It is important to see that such "rules of the game" can be either explicit or tacit, and can constitute as well as govern the activity. A constitutive rule defines what counts as play, what *constitutes* pitching, for instance. Pitching is not just throwing the ball toward the batter. It is doing so in certain ways with certain intentions. The constitutive intention or "rule" of pitching is "try to get the batter out." Other constitutive rules include the number of strikes required to get the batter out, the distance between the pitching mound and the plate, and so forth. The rules that *govern* pitching include rules about balking, about the misuse of foreign matter on the ball, and so forth.

Some rules, then, are used to regulate (govern) the playing of the game, and some are used to define (constitute) the game itself. Thus the rules of baseball not only tell us what we may and may not do when we are playing that game. They also tell us just what will and will not count as playing the game of baseball. In addition, they will provide a specialized and interrelated vocabulary, the meaning of which is determined by the rules. Moreover, the rules will only be describable in terms of this vocabulary. A hit in baseball is not the same thing as a hit in blackjack. A credit in college is not the same as a credit in a department store. One must understand the concept of a "hit" or a "credit" in terms of the rules that constitute the "game" as a whole. In other words, there is a circular relationship between the rules that constitute the game and the vocabulary in which the rules are stated. In order to understand the rules, written or unwritten, of any "game," one must have an understanding of the requisite vocabulary, and in order to understand the vocabulary, one must understand the rules.

This circular relationship requires a special form of understanding that we will discuss when we explore the concept of hermeneutics. However, the fact that individuals must understand the rules, vocabulary, conventions, and point of a "game" to be able to play it suggests that an acceptable analysis of social behavior must require due attention to such things. The rules and the vocabulary cannot exist in some abstract, impersonal realm. They must be understood by those who are engaged in the activity. This does not mean that any single individual, or even a group of individuals, must be able to recite all the rules. Rather, it means that they must be able to act and speak in such a way that the articulation of the rules would enable them and us to understand the sense that they make of their activity. In baseball, for example, it is an implicit understanding of the rules that allows us to draw the appropriate connections between hitting the ball and running the bases; and in school, the connection between listening to lectures and taking exams. This brings us to another key factor in the analysis of social behavior—the intentions and goals of the individuals who are engaged in specific activities. We need to know that the intentions of the agent are being structured in some significant way by a certain subset of the rules, as well as that the agent may be making free choices among alternatives allowed by the rules. For example, when the hitter swings the bat, we need to know whether he is doing so in order to get on base, help a teammate reach home plate, or both. When a child raises a hand in class, is it to get called on or to get lost in a sea of hands in hopes of avoiding the embarrassment of seeming not to know the answer? The case of "The New Student" in chapter 8 provides a classroom example of a teacher trying to figure out the social rules operating when a new student is unable to make friends. If you examine the case, you will see that it is not an easy thing to do.

Interpretive Scholarship in Education

Interpretive scholarship in education has tended to take two different forms, each of which is closely related to an aspect of the baseball example. One of these looks at the intentions and reasons of individuals in classroom contexts, while the other looks at the shared system of meanings found within a school. We have already seen that an analysis and interpretation of the participants' meaning has become an important component of some of the recent work in neo-Marxist educational scholarship. Willis's research clearly goes beyond the traditional orthodox Marxist account of schooling by taking the interpretive framework of the lads into account. He helps us to see and interpret schooling through the eyes of the lads. In this section we will look at work that has been developed independently of a Marxist framework and that demonstrates the significance of the interpretive point of view in understanding schooling as a social activity.

The discipline of anthropology has been especially important in the development of interpretive research programs within the field of education. Social anthropologists and ethnographers have stressed the importance of understanding the perspective of students, teachers, and others who are engaged in the educational enterprise. The ethnographers who study classroom behavior have been especially insistent that educational researchers should avoid imposing their own theories on those who are the objects of their study. The point of educational research, as the interpretivist sees it, is rather to understand the various meanings and "rules of the game" that constitute and govern the culture of the classroom and not to try to prove one general theory or another. In contrast to a functionalist, an interpretivist would not want to assess schooling in terms of some pre-established notion of progress and development. In

contrast to the Marxist, the interpretivist would insist that not all important educational activity can be explained in terms of class domination. In
fact, the interpretivist would remind both orthodox Marxists and functionalists that their own way of viewing classroom life is just one among
several plausible interpretations of the social and political dimensions of
schooling.

Ray McDermott, an interpretivist ethnographer who studies classroom behavior, provides, in a study done with Lois Hood, a very detailed
example of the way in which different roles and rules of the game may
operate in the classroom setting.[5] McDermott views the classroom as a
place where status and meaning are constantly negotiated in the process
of everyday interaction. Success and failure are the results of what he
calls the politics of everyday classroom life, as issues are negotiated
between different students and between the students and the teacher. In
this interaction the rules of the game are established and each of the
students comes to take on different roles within the game as it is defined
by the interaction of the various parties.

A vivid example of McDermott's approach can be found in his
observations of the lowest-level reading group in a primary school
classroom. To a person first observing this group, actions "typical" of
"low-level" readers might be noticed—fidgeting, distractedness, talking
out loud, and so on. It probably would seem that the teacher must
exercise firm control to keep the children on task. In his analysis of the
reading-group situation, however, McDermott stresses that the children
are seen to be "off task," not because there is something deficient in them
but because the observer is looking for the wrong task for them to be
attending to. Indeed, the students are quite attentive to their task at hand,
which, unfortunately, is better described as "playing the game that is
always played at reading time" than as "learning to read."

The "game" is a group encounter in which the actions of teacher and
students are guided by each other. The overt organization of the group is
based upon each child's reading a passage aloud. As one child finishes
reading a passage, all the other children raise their hands, and the teacher
calls on one of them to pick up where the previous reader left off. But it is
too simplistic to conclude that the teacher controls the group. At the end
of each reading turn there is a great deal of movement—hands go up, one
child tips back in his chair, another moves her head to avoid the teacher's
glance. The striking thing is that this apparent confusion constantly
recurs at the end of each reading turn. Far from being random, the
children's actions are under control. And this control is essentially inde-
pendent of explicit commands of the teacher. Rather, control is exercised
by all the group members as they take clues from and respond to the
behavior of each other.

This orchestration of movement is not merely the result of conditioning. When there are disruptions of the pattern, as when a disturbance occurs in another part of the classroom, the children look to each other and the teacher to determine how the group will respond. The important points to recognize are that all the "actors" are attuned to the group encounter and play their parts as developed in the group interaction. Furthermore, an observer must not bring preconceived notions about what is happening in the group (for example, assuming that reading is their shared task) but must examine the task as the group determines it.

A particular example may help illustrate these points. Rosa, a young child in the group, is its poorest reader. As the last reader is about to complete the passage and the other children are raising their hands, Rosa's eyes stay glued to the page and her body remains slumped over the book as everyone is bringing theirs to an erect posture. As the teacher scans the raised hands and starts to call on the next reader, Rosa's eyes begin to lift off the page. At the moment when the next reader is called upon and everyone else's eyes begin to return to the book, Rosa sits erect and raises her hand. In this way, McDermott observes, a subtle bargain between the teacher and Rosa is reinforced and sustained. While Rosa maintains the appearance of an interested, participating member of the group, the teacher does not embarrass Rosa by calling upon her to read. The other children accept the situation; the teacher's treatment of Rosa is not challenged, nor does Rosa lose face. The additional consequence, however, is that Rosa does not have many opportunities to learn how to read. But although Rosa would be considered a failure if one assessed her reading performance, her actions are a kind of backhanded achievement. Her goal was to minimize her embarrassment, and in this she was successful.

McDermott believes that too often educational researchers blame school failure either on the child for being intellectually deficient or on the teacher for having a biased attitude. He feels that a more fruitful approach would be to examine the interaction patterns in the classroom in order to understand the interpretive understandings that may be occurring. According to McDermott, the tendency to blame either the teacher or the child arises because most educational researchers make the mistake of viewing the individual as the primary unit of analysis and of ascribing certain traits, such as competence or incompetence, to individuals as such. Rosa would be a good case in point if we were to rate her on a standard reading test. However, for the interpretivist researcher, the classroom is a place where people do things together, and as McDermott and Hood assert, *"The proper unit of analysis for what people do together is what people do together."*[6] In other words, what the ethnographer is looking for are the social rules that structure individual behavior in a particular group setting. McDermott and Hood note that "the rules derived from our analysis are ideally the rules that the people have been using themselves to organize each other."[7]

McDermott and others have been interested in finding out the strategies that children use to deflect otherwise shameful exposure. Like Rosa, they may play at the game of participation while they also minimize, to whatever degree possible, the actual displays of incompetence. Other students hide their inadequate performance by eliciting the cooperation of friendly classmates who help cover up the display of incompetency. In still other cases, students wear their "nonreader" status as a badge that solidifies their identification with other, nonreading members of their peer group, as well as reinforcing the teacher's view of their inherent incompetence.[8]

For the interpretivist the object of study is to find out just what is going on in a specific social situation and to discover the meaning that it has for those who participate in it. The interpretivist does not ask whether some people are better than others in reading, writing, or mathematics. Rather, the task is to find the way in which different goals are nested together and to use this understanding to define the character of a specific social situation. In the case of the poor readers, for example, the significance given to their displays of incompetence leads them to adopt certain face-saving strategies. The way in which the two goals, learning to read and saving face, work together will help define the character of that classroom. Indeed, for McDermott it is a mistake to view competence as a property of individuals. He believes that competence is best understood as a property of situations. Situations are organized so that some kinds of behavioral displays take on more significance than others. A student may be competent in a whole range of activities except the ones that the school defines as significant. For this reason, McDermott suggests that we try to find the rational core behind any display of behavior.

We can develop this kind of understanding only by exploring the meanings that such behavior has for the actors themselves. One might inquire of McDermott's study whether such an exploration has been adequately developed. Since neither teachers nor students have been asked how they view their own actions, one might wonder about the correctness of the particular account that McDermott gives. Nevertheless, the general point remains quite sound. We need to know how participants understand their own situation before we begin to think about describing their behavior in more general terms. Whether or not we choose to ask the participants about this understanding will depend in part on how well we think they may be able to articulate it and whether we believe that they have reason to tell us the truth. We may feel that asking participants about the meaning that an event has for them is generally a good practice. However, we should not assume that the explication or communication of meaning is a simple task. In the following chapter we shall look at some complexities that are involved in the communication of meaning and some factors that may lead to miscommunication. Before going on you may want to consider the case "Mainstream or Not?" in chapter 8. It will provide an opportunity to consider the interpretivist point of view as well as the Marxist and functionalist.

Chapter 7

Meaning and Messages; Schooling and Socialization

We have seen that interpretivist or qualitative educational researchers are interested in exploring the ways individuals understand their social situations and act in them. The school as well as the classroom is a unit of analysis for these researchers. In his classic description of *Life in Classrooms*[1], Philip Jackson has provided a richly textured, insider's view of what goes on in elementary schools from a variety of research and commonsense perspectives. Even though his study shares some ground with functionalism, as we mentioned in our chapter 2 discussion of the "hidden curriculum," it also gets into the hearts and heads of students and teachers and helps us better understand their actions and their perceptions of schooling. In a similar way, Philip Cusick brought an interpretivist approach to his study of a high school.[2] He believes that an adequate understanding of any student's behavior cannot be gained through an examination of isolated features such as social class, age, or homelife. Rather, he argues that a study of the student's total environment has to be made. He immersed himself in a high-school environment for six months in order to study it. Similarly, Alan Peshkin studied the role that the schools play in the life of a community by participating in the ongoing activity of a community as it relates to its schools.[3]

Jackson's and Cusick's macrostudies of life in schools and Peshkin's studies of school–community relations underscore the importance interpretivists place on discovering and describing the implicit rules and understandings that govern people's behavior in a social setting. This suggests that what is being interpreted by the researcher are events that have already been preinterpreted by the participants. And what the participants interpret are the messages that are sent, received, and structured in a certain way in a particular social context. To understand more fully what goes on in classrooms and schools, then, we need to know more about how messages are sent and interpreted by people.

A message is the simplest unit of communication. A series of messages may be strung together to form a text, such as a novel, a lecture, or a theory. As the simplest unit of communication, a message is the vehicle through which meaning is delivered from one person to another. However, the message is different from the meaning in the sense that the same meaning can be delivered through different messages, and conflicting meanings can be delivered through the same message. I can tell you that I love you by saying the words, "I love you"; I can convey the same meaning by touching you in a certain kind of way or by glancing lovingly in your direction. Yet I could do any and all of these things and mean something quite different, as I would if we were performing *Romeo and Juliet* and I were intending to mean "this is the way that people behave when they are in love with one another." Or I could say, "I love you," in a tone that was dripping with sarcasm. A message and its meaning are tied together in important ways, but just as the package is not the present, the message is not the meaning.

One of the reasons that a message can be distinguished from its meaning is because there are at least three different kinds of meaning that can be transmitted by a message. A full interpretation of the message will often require an understanding of each of the three kinds of meaning and the way in which they fit together. The first kind of meaning can be called the *propositional* content of the message; its function is to make an explicit claim about some aspect of the world. The second kind may be called the *relational* content; its function is to indicate something about the relationship between the person delivering the message and the person receiving it. The third kind of meaning can be identified as the *attitudinal* content of the message; this tells us how the message is to be taken or the attitude that we should have toward it.

The propositional content of the message refers to the aspect of a communication that is the verbal substance of the message; it usually makes a truth claim. "It is raining outside," "John is a good student," "All bodies fall at the same rate of speed" are all examples of statements that make a truth claim. In each statement, there is not only a specific topic being addressed—such as the weather or John's ability and behavior—but also an implicit claim that there is some authoritative way in which to check the truth or falsity of the statements. "If you don't believe that it is raining outside, take a look" or "Go ahead and check John's grades and behavior." We can also transmit personal and valuative propositional meanings, as when we say, "I'm sad" or "That's a beautiful painting." In such cases authoritative tests are not so easy to come by. Even so, this is what most of us take communication to be about—sending propositional messages back and forth.

Now consider the following statement by a judge in a courtroom: "I order you to serve five years in prison and to pay a fine of $1,000." While this message is propositionally about a time and money penalty, there is another kind of message implied by this statement, one that asserts the relation of the judge to the defendant. The relational content of a message refers to the relative positions of the one who issues the message and the one who receives it. This aspect of the message may communicate something about the rights or responsibilities of the speaker and listener, or about the expectations that one party may properly have of the other. It may also communicate whether the speaker accepts the listener as an equal, a subordinate, or a superior, and whether as a member of the same group or a different group. The relational content is most obvious in statements that we call commands or promises, but it can be transmitted in less explicit ways. The decision to use a first or a last name in addressing another person is often a decision about what relational message is appropriate to send. The key feature of the relational content is its affirmation that a certain relationship between the speaker and the listener is appropriate. For example, for one person to command another is also to affirm the right of the speaker to issue orders in this situation and the duty of the listener to follow them. If you say to your younger sister or brother, "Put your books away," you make such an affirmation. And in the case of such things as commanding, sentencing, or promising, the speaker is also performing a social act beyond the mere communication of propositional meaning. Making a promise is doing something with words. It is committing oneself to some future act.[4]

The relational content may be communicated in a number of different ways. The most obvious involves an initial clause in which the speaker tells the listener what he is doing in uttering the sentence. "I require," "I order," "I suggest" are all examples in which the speaker affirms by words a certain relationship between himself and the listener. However, the relational content may be communicated in other ways as well. The tone of voice is one mode of communicating a relationship, as are the clothes or uniform one is wearing or the setting in which one chooses to have the message delivered. In a classroom, a teacher often sends many kinds of relational messages to establish his or her authority.

The attitudinal content of the message refers to the way in which the content communicated by the message is supposed to be taken. It refers to the feeling or attitude that is properly associated with a certain message. This aspect of a message may be communicated by words such as: "Isn't it sad that Sally is sick today?" However, as with the relational content, attitudinal content also may be communicated by tone of voice, expressions, gestures, and settings. For a speaker to say, "I love you," while performing in a play is to tell the listener *not* to take seriously these sincerely spoken words. To say to a student "Good work! You've come a long way!" is not just to make a substantive claim and assert your relation as teacher, but also to send a message of feeling and attitude. Could you imagine the meaning changing if, as a teacher, you said the same words to your principal?

Before going on, let us look at an example that illustrates how such complex messages can be interpreted differently by "insiders" and "outsiders." Knowing or guessing what game is being played leads to different interpretations of the same behavior. Consider the "insult game." A teacher hears her students insulting each other with name calling that makes her blush each day as she enters the classroom. She lectures them and finally turns to punishing them in an attempt to stop the use of abusive language. She has interpreted the propositional content literally as an insult, the relational content as indicating enemies standing toe-to-toe, and the attitudinal content as hatred and animosity. About to be punished, the offenders come to her to explain it is all in fun and not serious. The propositional content is just a ritualized set of words that do not literally mean anything, the relational content is friendship and friendly competition, and the attitude displayed is respect based on one's ability to play the game with believable but mock sincerity. Should she punish them? Is the game as harmless as the students think or as harmful as she thinks? How do we know when an interpretation is a misinterpretation?

The content of a message is often carried forward by the form and setting in which the message is delivered. The practice of "parent–teacher conferences" is one example of the way in which the setting and form of the narrative communicates the attitudinal content as well as the relational and the propositional. In this setting a statement like "Mary doesn't share with other children" is saying more than what is true about Mary's behavior in school. It communicates more than just propositional content and the teacher–parent relation. It also communicates just how the parent should feel about what Mary has not been doing. Even more importantly, it reinforces certain social norms about what is proper and what is improper for a person to do. In other words, the teacher's statement about Mary is not just a description and an implicit judgment that this child's behavior is inappropriate. It is also an affirmation of a certain concept of a good community spirit. Indeed, the statement about Mary can only be taken as a negative judgment if such notions of what is required for good community spirit are already in place and serve as shared social norms. In this instance communication is possible because those norms are understood by each party, and it goes along smoothly, without interruption, when each party to the message shares those norms. If, however, the listener had recently arrived from another culture or belonged to a subculture unfamiliar with the norm of sharing, the significance of the conversation would be puzzling. If the norm is unknown to the listener, then there is confusion about the point of the discussion. If, however, the listener is not a stranger and is familiar with the norm but disagrees with it, then communication is disrupted in another way. The listener's attention does not flow with the speaker's. Instead of participating in the judgment about Mary, the listener may begin to pass judgment on the speaker. The speaker may be deemed "an enemy of rugged individualism" or "against private property." The attitudinal framework in which the conference was set has been disrupted because the background norms of the discussion are no longer shared.

In this section, we have seen how messages can be more than words; they carry with them propositional, relational, and attitudinal meanings. From the interpretivist point of view, we are each and all social beings who learn to negotiate our way in social situations in which we share background knowledge and meanings with others, interpret the situations we are in terms of the "rules" in operation (which we often have a hand in making), and act in terms of our intentions and understandings. The key to being able to do all this is being able to interpret. Human beings have been interpreting since language began, but in more recent times scholars have tried to develop a "science" of interpretation called "hermeneutics."

Hermeneutics and Interpretation

We have already raised the question of the validity of using a natural-science stance in the study of the social world. In twentieth-century thought about the nature of social science, a hermeneutics approach was advocated by such thinkers as Wilhelm Dilthey, Hans-Georg Gadamer, and Paul Ricouer. Hermeneutics is the science of interpretation. It traditionally describes a sophisticated, higher level of understanding. Thus biblical scholars engage in hermeneutics when they are interpreting a passage in a sacred text, and legal scholars engage in hermeneutics when they try to clarify the intent of a certain law. However, a similar process is involved when a youngster tries to understand and behave according to the norms of his or her classroom, or when an anthropologist tries to comprehend the ways of a foreign culture. Hermeneutics involves a reading and interpretation of some kind of "human text." However, the terms "reading" and "text" need to be defined generously.

The "text" of our social world is complex. It is made up of many parts, each with its own set of rules, norms, concepts, and roles that constitute a particular form of social activity. Those who advocate a hermeneutics approach to research take the social scientist's problem to be one of finding a good interpretation of human action that is based on an understanding of the rules, roles, and norms that are operative in the social situation. Understanding the parts helps with understanding the whole of a complex social system, and understanding the whole helps make sense of parts and their relation to each other and to the whole. As we have seen, schools have been investigated as such complex social systems by interpretivist educational researchers, and the rule-governed behavior of students, teachers, and administrators has been described.

The problem of "good" interpretation, however, is crucial. Rules and canons for good interpretations have been developed in the hermeneutic tradition, but there is a general recognition that there is no such thing as *the* correct or *the* one and only possible interpretation. However, this does not mean that one interpretation is as good as another. An interpretation is like a hypothesis, a sophisticated guess that things will turn out a certain way if tested. An interpretation is "tested" against the facts of the social "text," and as more and more of the "text" is "read," the interpretation becomes more or less "validated," more or less "probably" correct. This all happens within a hermeneutic circle.

The term *hermeneutic circle* refers both to the process whereby we come to an understanding of a given social text and to the process that we might use to choose between two or more competing interpretations of the same text. The process is called the hermeneutic *circle* to indicate that in the interpretation of a text, there is nothing beyond the unfolding text itself to which an appeal can be made. We must stay within the boundaries of the text itself to interpret it on its own terms. If, for example, you were reading a detective story, you would appeal to the text to support your guess that the butler did it until you recall or come across some new information in the text (perhaps you find out the butler was really away on his day off); then you reject your "plausible" interpretation and search for another. You do not consult the daily newspaper. You stay within the text. In other words, we understand a piece of the text by appealing to the framework and meaning of the whole text, and we come to understand the whole text by exploring the meaning and structure of its various parts.

Consider another example, that of a judge trying to interpret a particular law in order to apply it in a certain case. To support an interpretation, the judge will only be able to appeal to the facts of the case, to a body of relevant laws, and to their ongoing interpretations by legal scholars and other judges within the judicial system. If the judge wishes to "uncover" the intent of the law, he cannot go to the lawmakers and ask what they might have been thinking when they drew up the legislation. The lawmakers may no longer be alive, or if alive, may never have conceived of the kind of case that is now being addressed. In deciding which law applies to a specific case, and in interpreting and applying the law, a judge appeals only to the body of laws and to their ongoing application and interpretation. Note, however, that *this* law and the way in which it is interpreted in *this* case will become a part of the body of laws that comprises the legal tradition. Other judges, deciding other cases, will then have access to this interpretation as they render subsequent decisions. In other words, a particular law must be understood in terms of the body of laws that comprises the legal tradition as a whole. However, the legal tradition can only be understood in terms of the particular laws that comprise it. This movement from the whole to its parts and back to the whole again represents the idea of the hermeneutic circle. It is this process that interpretivists believe will make for "good" interpretation and for a sensitive social science.

In a similar manner, if we were to try to interpret the human text of a school, as some researchers have done, then we would have to look at the relation of parts to whole in the school—not in some mechanical way, but in a dynamic, interactive way that would lead us to a fuller and richer understanding of the actual life going on in classrooms. As we saw at the beginning of this chapter, Jackson and Cusick were among the first educational researchers to do this. We turn now to some of the aspects of schooling that have been described by functionalists and Marxists and consider them from an interpretivist point of view.

Interpretation and Socialization

Interpretation is usually thought of as the engagement of a single person with a written text. Many of the activities associated with interpretation, however, are also entailed in the process of socialization. Unfortunately, socialization is often depicted as a passive process of imprinting and habituation, and the active, interpretive element is lost. This is certainly the case in much of the functionalist literature on schooling, and in some of the orthodox Marxist literature as well. In this literature, socialization is taken to be the process by which new members of the group come to acquire the habits, attitudes, or beliefs of the older members. In contrast to this passive account of socialization, it is important to note that well-socialized members of a group need not share all the attitudes and beliefs of the other members, and there may in fact be much behavioral variation among already socialized members. What is shared is a structure of intelligibility that enables communication and intersubjective understanding to take place and provides a foundation for shared commitments to be expressed.

Suppose that we return to our now familiar example of the social scientist studying American baseball in order to see just what is entailed by an interpretivist view of socialization. Suppose that our social scientist decides not to go home after all but stays and actually learns about the game of baseball; and suppose that this time she is successful. In other words, she learns the concepts and distinctions that are relevant to baseball; she learns the vocabulary that is necessary to talk intelligently about the game, and she learns the rules that one is required to know in order to play the game or to follow others when they are playing it. She has thus developed a structure of intelligibility that is shared by all of those who know baseball. (You might think analogously of a student from a foreign country who attends and "learns" a new school system and extend that example as you read on.)

Of course, this knowledge does not mean that our scientist has yet been socialized in any complete way. She may know *about* baseball but may detest the game. While the shared structure of intelligibility is an important component of socialization, it is only a part of the process. Suppose, however, that her experience with baseball begins to go beyond her role as an impartial social scientist. Suppose that she actually begins to enjoy watching the game. She starts to go to the ballpark regularly, and often does so without her calculator. She starts to follow the progress of different teams, begins to root for a certain one, starts to criticize the manager for making bad trades, and argues with some of the team's loyal supporters about the merits of this or that decision. At this point she has done more than simply develop a structure of shared intelligibility. She can do more than recognize a game when she sees one and use the vocabulary that is called "baseball talk" to interpret and communicate with others. She has come to structure her own wants and inclinations in line with a certain level of participation in the game. She has become a baseball fan.

While the development of a shared structure of intelligibility does not complete the process of socialization, it is a necessary condition for it to take place, and the development of this structure is very much like the activity of interpretation. It involves the learning of an appropriate set of rules, conceptual distinctions, and relationships, and it involves learning how to speak and listen in terms of these. In addition it involves knowing what it means for people to structure their own inclinations and activities according to these concepts, distinctions, and relations. Socialization takes the process one step further. In addition to knowing what it means for a person to structure his or her own inclinations and activity according to certain rules, a person also begins to actually structure his or her own desires and activities according to those rules. There is, however, an element of freedom here. Not everyone who learns about baseball becomes a fan. Not everyone who shares structures of social intelligibility must actively participate in their use. The deterministic quality of functionalist and orthodox Marxist interpretations is opened up to human freedom and will from the interpretivist point of view.

Along this same line, imagine a classroom and your own experience as a student in it. You know the rules, written and unwritten, for participating. There are propositional, relational, and attitudinal messages being sent between fellow students, teacher and students, students and the teacher. You know what you are about because you grasp the point of the many activities going on. You choose to participate or not and invent strategies for getting on or getting through. The manifest content of the classroom is the propositional meaning contained in the formal content of the subject matter. You feel that if you learn it (some history, some math, some science), you will be better able to understand, interpret, and act in the world you live in with others; at least your teacher tells you that. You sense all the other messages being sent and received, though, and participate in the social activity we call schooling as a more or less free-acting, autonomous, social individual. Lyn Corno offers a description of the practical value of what we have been imaginatively describing. She calls it "classroom literacy."

> We can define classroom literacy more specifically as a process of coming to know *the commonly acknowledged structures and functions of classrooms and of being able to use this knowledge productively in the social and academic roles that classrooms define.* Students who are literate about classrooms are also likely to be literate about themselves—both as learners and as social beings. They are likely to be able to cope with the kinds of social and academic blocks or difficulties commonly encountered in classrooms—to be able to handle such blocks adaptively. If students can be helped to become literate about classrooms early in their school careers, they stand a better chance of using this information as they cross the bridges from pre-K and kindergarten to elementary school, and beyond. They stand in good position to change aspects of classroom experiences they can change, to handle those experiences they cannot change, and to view their experiences in school somewhat differently as a result. As Richard deCharms suggested, there is great power in believing that one is an "origin" of the events in one's life, and not a "pawn" in someone else's game.[5]

This is how the interpretivist sees the relation of school and society, not as class conflict and legitimation, nor as functional socialization, selecting, and training, but as the development of a shared social structure of intelligibility. If you would like to consider further the issue of free agency in a cultural-educational context as it has been posited here, see the dispute over "Social Conditioning and Freedom" in chapter 8.

Interpretation, Socialization, and Legitimation

Another way to look at the interpretivist perspective is as a point of view that provides a new way to interpret, clarify, and sharpen the central issues that separate the Marxist and functionalist positions. To illustrate how interpretivism may help clarify the nature of the conflict between the functionalist and the Marxist points of view, we need to recall that there are two important elements in an interpretivist analysis. The first is to be found at the social level and involves the meanings, rules, and norms through which a certain society is constituted. The second is to be found on the individual level and involves the way in which a person's inclinations and wants become structured through social learning.

Functionalists who have looked at schooling as society's neutral instrument of socialization into the patterns of thought and behavior required by an industrial world have focused on factors that largely involve the structuring of individual wants and inclinations. In doing so, they have analyzed the way in which industrial society "necessarily" requires that schools take over the socializing function from the family in ways that enable individuals to adapt to the larger social world of mass society. Industrialization and the growth of technology are perceived as inevitable, governed by their own rules of development; the school is given the function of structuring the wants and inclinations of individuals according to the habits and skills they need to function effectively in an ever more technologically integrated society. Because technological growth is perceived as an inevitable process of development, this body of literature focuses upon the need to restructure the wants and inclinations of individuals in ways that will be compatible with this interpretation of reality.

Marxists, who claim that the schools are largely involved in legitimizing existing inequalities, focus their attention on a different aspect of the educational process, based on a different interpretation of contemporary social reality. They draw attention to class relations and to the nature of the social meanings and rules that children learn to adopt. Their interpretation highlights the way in which social roles are generated in contemporary society, providing some people with great power and authority, while restricting the opportunities for power and position available to others. The Marxist study of schooling thus focuses on the way in which children are taught to accept a situation of reduced authority and constricted opportunity.

The concept of legitimation, as it is used by Marxists, covers much of the same propositional ground as does the concept of socialization when used by functionalists. Each refers to a process whereby children learn to adopt the values and behavior patterns that are required to live in the modern social world. Nevertheless, while there is similarity in the propositional content of these two concepts, there is a great deal of difference in the attitudinal content. School "socialization" for the functionalist is essential to growing up in a modern technological society. It serves the individual child well. "Legitimation" for the Marxist is essential only for maintaining the source of class domination. It serves not the individual child, but the ruling elite and the structure that supports them. Hence, whereas the functionalist views technology as a basically benign engine serving to create individual opportunities, the Marxist sees class domination as a malignant social force, over which the individual has little or no control and which serves to generate inequalities and to reduce opportunities. Each takes a different element of the interpretivist view of the social world as its point of departure.

When the functionalists claim the schools serve to socialize children into the behavior required by an ever more technical world, they have little doubt that the children are learning to conform to rules that *really do* govern social and economic life. Teach a child that "it is not who you know but what you know that counts" and you have presumably taught that child a fundamental principle of contemporary social life. For the Marxists, things are quite different. The basic idea behind their concept of legitimation is that children are systematically taught to misunderstand the rules of the game. Tell them that "it is not who you know but what you know that counts" and you have told them a lie. Yet according to the Marxists, the system can only work if the lies are believed and the nature of the real rules remain misunderstood. In this way, the Marxists believe, the schools exercise an essential role in maintaining the present system. They provide the systematic misrepresentation of the rules that is required to maintain inequality and domination. If people were to become aware of the real rules, the nature of the game would change. The functionalists believe that children are learning the real rules of the game, while the Marxists believe that students are being taught to structure their inclinations and intentions according to the rules of one game, while another game is really being played. Marxists also believe that continuation of the real game depends upon the fact that people persist in misunderstanding its rules. This interpretation of the differences between the two approaches helps us to see and raise the basic interpretivist question: What really are the rules of the game in a modern democratic society?

Once again, we seem to be required to discover the true view of the rules of the game. Instead of doing that, however, there is another tack the interpretivist might take in this dispute; that is, to try to explicate the constitutive rules for a democratic society and to urge that they be consciously and deliberately taught to each new generation of future citizens. The liberal political theorist Amy Gutman offers one version of this strategy in *Democratic Education*.[6] She sees our democratic society as essentially one where "we [can] disagree over the relative value of freedom and virtue, the nature of the good life, and the elements of moral character [but nevertheless we share] a common commitment . . . to collectively recreating [this open] society we share."[7] She urges us to consciously reproduce such a democratic form of life that permits disagreement and that is constituted from such virtues, principles, attitudes, and values as freedom, tolerance, reasonableness, justice, equality, open-mindedness, nondiscrimination, and nonrepression. Her view of social reproduction is neither the functionalist's deterministic socialization nor the Marxist's hegemonic, unconscious legitimation; she argues for the conscious and intentional attempt to reproduce the kind of society we want to live in. Of course, being human, we can fail to accomplish what we set out to do. There is no fundamental determinism in the interpretivist view.

Objections to the Interpretivist Approach

When the interpretivist point of view is presented as more than simply a way of clarifying certain issues and is put forward as a more adequate way of understanding social and educational life, however, new controversies emerge. Interpretivism is often advanced as a way to counter what is seen to be the overly mechanical and deterministic model that is found in certain forms of both functionalism and Marxism. Instead of offering a strictly causal account of social life, it provides an account in which individual reason and cultural rules are given a primary role. Instead of searching for universal laws that are thought applicable to all forms of society, it emphasizes rule-governed behavior, a degree of individual autonomy, and the uniqueness of local situations. And instead of emphasizing the need to verify interpretations against an "objective" world, the interpretive approach stresses the importance of understanding and validating interpretations in their own contextual terms. In educational research, the quantitative–qualitative debate mirrors these differences.

The objections to interpretivism as a superior mode of understanding are many, and here we will mention only a few of them. Neither orthodox Marxists nor functionalists would necessarily object to the interpretivist point of view unless it were assumed that social rules, norms, and interpretations could not be explained by more fundamental causal mechanisms. Functionalists would tend to identify these mechanisms with the level of development of a specific society, while Marxists would include in their explanation the relationship that different classes have to the means of production.

While both functionalists and Marxists might see the need to understand how a certain group views its world, neither would accept the idea that this is the primary function of social research. In contrast to the view that we should avoid attributions of incompetence to social actors, both functionalists and Marxists, for different reasons, would find such an attribution important. Functionalists need the category of incompetence to explain and justify the different social positions that students will come to occupy after they leave school. Marxists need the same category to identify and explain false consciousness. Whereas both might agree with the interpretivist that there is a need to understand the particular interpretation developed by social actors, they would insist upon the need to apply a more refined set of procedures in order to judge its adequacy. Functionalists, for example, would judge inadequate any interpretation they thought was based upon a commitment to particularistic norms, while Marxists would view with suspicion any interpretation developed in the context of class domination.

Finally, both functionalists and Marxists would object to what they perceive as an inconsistent relativism in the interpretivists' position. Interpretivism seems to be asserting the need to understand all perspectives on their own terms. This seems to require that we put aside our own standards of judgment and enter the world of those we are studying. This perspective also seems to imply that all perspectives are equally worthwhile and that we will do well to understand and to tolerate each of them. Yet when it comes to the question of the adequacy of different theoretical perspectives, there is little doubt that those who argue for the interpretive point of view look upon both Marxism and functionalism as inferior forms of understanding. Thus, on the one hand, the attractiveness of this perspective is to be found in its acceptance of other points of view, while, on the other hand, it seems to affirm that there is at least one point of view that is more acceptable than any other, and, of course, that view is the interpretivist one.

What Is at Stake?

At this point, you might well be asking "Just what is at stake in taking one of these approaches?" Granted, they provide different ways to think about schools, but do they have any implications for the way in which schools work in our society, and for your role as a teacher in the educational process? The answer to this question depends on how you think about *your* role. If you believe that your role as a teacher is simply to do what you are told, then these theories may not make a significant difference. However, if you believe that part of your responsibility as a citizen in a democratic society is to participate in determining what the goals of education should be, and if you also believe that your role as a teacher is to reflect on the worth of the means available to accomplish those goals, then these theories may influence how you define success and failure in schooling and, subsequently, what you are willing to work to achieve.

Consider recent attempts by the federal government to rationalize education. Historically, the control and financing of public education has largely been left to the states and local communities. However, federal interest in education began to grow in the last two decades of the twentieth century, especially in response to foreign economic competition. In the early 1980s, a report issued by President Reagan's Secretary of Education blamed schools for a weakened economy, alleging the schools had failed to produce an adequately trained workforce. The report, entitled *A Nation at Risk*, called for more rigorous academic standards in order to meet the economic challenge coming from overseas.

At the beginning of the twenty-first century, American schooling has been dominated by the creation and enforcement of policies aimed at holding schools accountable for reaching certain benchmark scores on standardized tests. One example is the No Child Left Behind Act of 2002, which rewards and punishes schools according to the performance of their students on such tests. One could agree or disagree with such federal policies from the point of any one of the three theories presented in this book. Moreover, we believe that these theories do influence the reasons for agreement or disagreement.

For example, some functionalists might agree with such test-based policies on the grounds that there is an important relationship between student achievement and the ability of a nation to compete with other nations economically. However, the other functionalists might disagree, pointing to the stagnation of the Japanese economy and the growth of the United States' economy during much of the 1990s, along with the relatively minor changes in the standardized test scores of children in the two nations during this time. These two functionalists would argue that such data is proof that the relationship between test scores and economic competitiveness is more complex than originally thought and that high-stakes testing may not be the best solution. In either case, however, both sets of functionalists would implicitly accept the idea that the goal of schooling is to advance economic competitiveness.

Conflict theorists, on the other hand, might take a more critical stance toward this assumed goal of schooling. They would likely challenge any claim that it was reached by a consensus and would ask about the people whose voices might have been left out of the deliberations or about the people whose interests the "consensus" really serves. In raising these questions, conflict theory provides an opening where other interests can enter; for example, labor interests, educators' interests, environmental and global interests, and so forth. An awareness of these other interests sometimes serves to aid in the formation of coalitions that may challenge official definitions of success and failure in school.

Lastly, interpretivist theorists would consider local conditions that affect the way federal and state mandates are interpreted and reconstructed by administrators, teachers, and students. For example, a high-stakes test that determines whether a school is rewarded or punished assumes that each student who is tested at the end of the year has been a student at the same school during the entire school year. In some schools, however, there is a large student turnover, and administrators and teachers at such schools might seek ways to prevent this from impacting the school's test scores, even if it means encouraging newer and slower students to stay home on the day of the tests. From an outsider's perspective this is cheating, but from the local perspective it is a method of correcting a perceived problem of inequity. Also, some teachers may interpret the mandates as a welcome call for higher standards while others may see them as forcing teachers to teach to the test and as limiting their time and ability to provide a richer curriculum. Thus, the interpretivist view reveals the local conditions that drive the reinterpretation of these mandates and allows for a more nuanced judgment about what is seen as serving the best interests of the children in any given school.

These examples should help you understand the relevance of these three theories for making sense of current practices and policies in schools. Not only do these theoretical stances help us understand how schools work, they also reveal new perspectives and provide different vocabularies that can help to ensure a fuller evaluation of the performance of schools. In the process, they open up avenues for discussion among the many different interests that impact our schools and provide each of us with the tools to address the influence of the powerful in our society.

We invite you to think about these fundamental issues in the chapter that follows. Of course, we really hope you will continue to think about such issues throughout your career as an educator. The last three offerings in chapter 8, "Interpretation and Epistemic Relativism," "A Third-World School System," and "The Curriculum," raise basic questions about the interpretivist point of view and contrast the three viewpoints presented in this book against each other.

Part V

CASES AND DISPUTES

Chapter 8

Cases and Disputes

We have examined three basic approaches to explaining and understanding the relation of schooling to society and have asked you to think about them along the way. They each have much to commend them as useful conceptualizing devices for getting at otherwise invisible forces possibly at work in the daily business of schooling. To help you develop and use the perspectives we have offered in this book, this last chapter contains a series of realistic vignettes—in the form of cases, dialogues, and disputes—that raise a number of issues not dealt with extensively or directly in the text. As you read them, think about the issues imbedded in them and discuss them with others. We think you will see why the ability to probe into basic aspects of the relation of schooling to society can make a difference in the ways teachers and administrators act. We think you will also see that we have not been dealing with esoteric theories that have no relation to reality. The cases and disputes that follow clearly show that the individual and collective practices of all educators, yourself included, can and do have lasting effects on the lives of persons and on the society in which we all live. As professional educators, we believe that we all have a responsibility to consider, monitor, and when morally appropriate, alter those effects. These cases and disputes are designed to help you become more sensitive to this dimension of the role of a responsible, professional educator.

To give you an overview of the topics we have treated and the major points at issue in them, we have provided a summary (see table 1) from which you can select cases and disputes of special interest to you. Of course, we could neither treat all the possible topics and issues nor anticipate those that would be of central social concern when you are using this text. So you should feel free to write your own cases and disputes or to bring up issues from your own experiences in your class discussions.

Some of you may have already sampled these cases and disputes by following the suggestions we made in each chapter. To indicate our recommendations of issues related to specific chapters, in table 1 we have placed a chapter number in parenthese following the title of each topic and issue listed. Of course, you should feel free to use them in any order suitable to your interests and purposes. Many of these cases and disputes also reach beyond the issues raised in the chapters, demonstrating that the real world of education is not as neatly packaged as the textbooks describing its basic dimensions. We hope you will use these cases and disputes as a bridge to the real world in which you will become a thinking and responsible professional educator.

TABLE 1. Summary of Cases and Disputes

Page	Title*	Major Issue
117	Student Government (1)	How do students learn to be "good citizens"?
119	The Roots of School Failure (1)	What really constitutes school success?
121	The Hidden Curriculum (2)	What do school materials teach?
122	National Reports on Education (2)	Are schools instruments of the state?
123	The Geography Lesson (2)	Should politics enter the classroom?
124	Resource Allocation (2)	What are the priorities of schools?
126	College or Workforce? (3)	How are the "best interests" of students determined?
128	Individual Differences and Equal Opportunity (3)	Can "equal" and "different" be resolved?
129	Social Reproduction (3)	What aspects of society do schools reproduce?
131	Equal but Separate (4)	Do school standards maintain the separation of social classes?
132	Education for Work (4)	Is a liberal education the best education?
133	Workforce School (4)	Can practical schooling limit opportunities?
134	Class Bias? (5)	Do teachers treat children from different backgrounds unfairly?
136	Social Studies (5)	Does hard work pay off?

* A number in parentheses after a title indicates that the case or dispute is recommended for use with that specific chapter.

Page	Title*	Major Issue
136	Interpretation and Ethical Relativism (5)	Can an interpretivist hold ethical standards?
137	The New Student (6)	Do foreign students have to change their ways to fit in?
138	Mainstream or Not? (6)	Is chronic misbehavior a handicap, and how should it be treated?
140	Social Conditioning and Freedom (7)	If home and school condition us, how free are we?
141	Interpretation and Epistemic Relativism (7)	Are some interpretations better than others?
142	A Third-World School System (7)	Can incompatible views be resolved in practice?
143	The Curriculum (7)	What approach best explains the traditional curriculum?

Student Government

Yorkville Middle School is located in an upper-class suburb of a large city. The great majority of students come from the affluent homes in the immediate neighborhood, but there are a few children from middle- and lower-income families who are bused in from the edge of the community.

The school lacks nothing in equipment and materials. The parents' largess extends to their children, too. Whether clothes, toys, or other gadgets (seemingly without regard for expense), the neighborhood children always have the latest trendy items. Those who bus in from outside the community are sometimes envious, sometimes ashamed of their own clothes and possessions, but always thankful for the great facilities available to them at Yorkville. The children are taught by their parents to value the society that has been so good to them.

Lessons in citizenship are considered to be important components of the Yorkville experience, and these are taught through school activities such as athletic teams, a school service program, and a student government. Alice Schwartz has been teaching at Yorkville for a number of years and has just accepted the unpaid position of faculty advisor to the student government. She has always considered herself a friend of the students and generally identifies with their interests. Alice also has very strong feelings about what the student government should accomplish. She envisions it as a rallying point for bringing the student body together as a community. It should serve the school community and contribute meaningfully to charities. She also sees it as an exercise in independence and responsibility for the students, an experiencing of democratic ideals.

Alice was very happy to see the enthusiasm demonstrated by candidates and other students during the first election held under her supervision. Some enterprising campaigners had posters and buttons printed up by a local company. Enthusiasm was further reflected by the often outlandish proposals and promises made during the candidates' speeches.

Once the election was over, though, Alice soon found that the vigor shown by the winning candidates before balloting did not carry over into real work as representatives. She is disappointed in the lack of initiative shown by the members of the student government. One representative even fails to come regularly to meetings.

One activity that was decided on and that pleased Alice is the continuation of the student body sponsorship of a foster child. The student government treasury contains $1,000 from the previous year and the P.T.A. has also contributed some money. But at a cost of $200 per month for sponsoring the child, the money will soon be gone, and so the student government has decided to hold a dance as a fund-raising activity.

School dances have always been one of the big money-makers at Yorkville and are generally well attended. This time, the Dance Committee has decided to make the dance something special by hiring a professional disc jockey and light show at a cost of $500. This expense casts doubt on the possibility of making any profit from the dance. The Dance Committee claims that the project will break even if $5, rather than the traditional $1.50, is charged for admission. Alice argued that the committee's plan missed the point of the activity—raising money for charity. One representative suggested that $5 was too much for some of the students to pay. When it came to a vote, though, the Dance Committee's plan was adopted by a wide margin.

Reflecting on her experiences as faculty adviser to this point, Alice feels that the group has failed to learn some important lessons about citizenship.

If you were Alice, what would you do? What have the students at Yorkville learned about representative government? Do the election campaign and the dance decision reflect the values of the Yorkville community? How do students learn to be "good, responsible citizens"?

The Roots of School Failure

Imagine yourself sitting in on the following discussion among four teachers in a faculty room at the end of the day:

A: My lowest math group really isn't doing well. I wish I knew what to do with them.

B: There are plenty of remediation materials in the resource center. You probably can find something there to help develop the skills your students are lacking.

C: Remediation is no answer. Look at the students in the group; they're mostly lower-class kids. That's where the source of the problem lies. The children don't succeed because the criteria of success are set by the upper classes. All your remediation program will do is serve to reinforce the children's conceptions of themselves as incapable, that they deserve their class situations.

B: You're right, they are lower-class kids, but you're selling them short. The source of the problem is not their class situation, but that they are at a disadvantage experientially. We as teachers can make up for that. Every child has the potential to succeed in school, and they can succeed if only we teachers are sensitive to their needs and abilities.

C: You've missed my point. A few disadvantaged kids will always succeed and so preserve the myth of the school's functionality. But the fact is that those who succeed are the ones able to demonstrate the traits that the upper classes value. And those aren't the values communicated in the home life and work life of the working classes. The large majority of these kids will end up as failures and be cycled into the same sorts of situations their parents endured. And then they will send their children to school to learn that they, too, are less capable, need remediation, and can aspire to only the worst jobs. The cycle never ends.

D: Wait a minute! Are you implying that lower-class children can't be successful in this society? If so, then you and *B* are both suffering from the same mistaken interpretation of success. It sounds like you both consider the ability to manipulate symbols and store knowledge to be the only criteria for success. From that assumption *B* concludes that most students can be successful if we teach them well while *C* argues that some students will never be successful no matter what we do. I believe that the root of school failure lies in what we consider meaningful success to be. Isn't a kid who can make change at a store successful in arithmetic even if he can't manipulate algebraic symbols on paper or remember abstract formulas?

C: So you want to say that being able to make change is being successful?! Is that going to get the person a fulfilling job that will provide a decent living? Or will it just qualify him for the most dull and servile jobs? Your solution is a middle-class cop-out.

D: No, it isn't. Once people understand that *they* define success and that our society has been too narrow in what is valued, people will see value in themselves and in others where it wasn't recognized before. Then people will recognize the need for change and fight for it.

C: Changes in values will come only after economic injustices have been eliminated. That will only come with the destruction of the capitalist system and its inherent repression of humane values. The teacher's job is to resist the curriculum imposed by the dominant classes and raise consciousness of its injustice.

B: The point is not to change our economic system or our conception of success. Both present the potential for everyone to enjoy a good life. We must help everyone achieve access to the best the system has to offer for the benefit of both individuals and the society. The teacher's job is to teach the school curriculum effectively and give everyone an equal chance to learn and rise through the system.

D: No. The point is to realize that our human condition is not determined by our access to some "system." It's determined in our interactions with people. People aren't cogs in a machine. The solution to social injustice is neither to shape the cog to the machine (*B*'s view) nor to shape the machine to the cog (*C*'s view). Those views are both too mechanistic. There are many criteria by which a worthwhile life can be measured. Everyone has valuable assets to bring to society. It is up to society to respect and reward all people as individuals. With that attitude, no one need be looked on as a failure and undeserving of the benefits that are their due.

A: Thanks a lot! It's been an interesting philosophical discussion. But I still have a problem—what am I to do when I meet with those kids at 10:00 tomorrow to teach them multiplication? I'm not sure anything any of you have said helps me at all or makes any difference.

Do you think that if any of these views are correct, it should make a difference in what teachers do? Does any one of these arguments make more sense to you than the others? Is there a functionalist, a conflict theorist, and an interpretivist here? What advice would you give *A*?

The Hidden Curriculum

In the past American schools were fortunate in receiving broad support for their efforts. In addition to tax revenue or tuition income, our schools benefited from volunteer services, philanthropic organizations, and the support of the business community. Help from outsiders often enabled the teacher to improve the curriculum and enrich our children's educational experiences without overburdening already strained budgets.

Clarence Darrow Junior High School has relied upon support from outside sources in many ways. Over the years, the library collection has been expanded by annual donations from the Free Enterprise Institute. The Institute usually selects books that espouse the virtues of rugged individualism and support traditional American values: biographies of men who succeeded through hard work and pluck, patriotic stories from American history, and positive accounts of family life. Representatives of the Free Enterprise Institute feel that this sort of educational material is of inestimable value for the protection of our freedom and the preservation of the American way.

The school's audio-visual department has benefited from corporate interest and contributions. Local offices of the telephone and power companies have supplied films and slide presentations on a variety of subjects: health, science, technology, and modern life. These visual aids bring information into the classroom that the teachers by themselves could never offer. The films are very popular among the students and have made lessons more pertinent for them. The teachers use the company films often.

John Robbins, a new teacher at Clarence Darrow, is encouraged by his principal to take advantage of these resources. But John, being a reflective and somewhat cautious person, decides he wants to take a close look at the various materials rather than use them naively. He views a utility company film on nuclear energy. The film, he decides, emphasizes the benefits and potential of nuclear power but does not address health and safety problems. John concludes that, besides the information given, the film conveys a hidden lesson, a biased espousal of the values and interests of the utility company without regard for the dangers to society. He decides not to use the film.

Is John's judgment about the message of the film justified? Is he right not to show the film? What about the functional value of the library books?

National Reports on Education

A: The new President's Commission on Education has made it clear in its reports that we are falling behind in the production of engineers and basic scientists compared to other modern nations. Our capacity to invent, do research, and provide the base for high-tech industry is eroding, and we soon will become a second-rate power unless the schools do something about it.

B: But the schools as they now function are part of the problem. They are lax on requirements. Students are given too much freedom and choose easier courses over math and science. We need to tighten standards and go back to requiring three years of math and three of science for high school graduation. We need to make the high school diploma stand for something again.

C: But what about students who aren't academically inclined? Do they have to meet those stiff requirements, too, even though they won't go on to college or try to become scientists and engineers? That's not fair.

B: Sure it is. Fair is giving everyone a chance to meet the requirements. It's unfair to give everyone the same diploma when some take hard courses and some take all the easy ones. A diploma should mean something and mean the same thing for everybody.

A: You're both focusing on the wrong issue. To get needed scientists and engineers, we have to provide incentives and develop accurate testing instruments to screen out the untalented from the talented, not require everybody to take stiff math and science courses. Find and reward the talented with government scholarships in math, science, and engineering, and you'll solve the problem.

C: But is it right to use the schools as instruments of national policy to solve the problems of private industry?

A: Why not? That's what they are, aren't they, instruments of the state? Whether we use them to produce good citizens or good engineers, it's all the same. The proper function of the schools is to serve society's needs.

C: But what happens when the perceptions of those needs change every few years? Must the schools change overnight? And what about the needs of the individual? Where do they come in?

B: What's good for the nation is good for the individual!

C: Always?

Is it always? Are the schools the instrument of society? Does functionalism preclude concern for individual needs?

The Geography Lesson

Margaret Baker teaches the sixth grade at Whittier Elementary School. Ms. Baker values citizen involvement in public affairs, and she is very active in several organizations, including the teachers' union, the Democratic party, and the American Civil Liberties Union. She sometimes uses classroom subject matter as a vehicle to explore and illuminate political issues for her students. In Ms. Baker's opinion, the need for an educated citizenry requires an introduction to political matters at an early age.

The sixth grade has been studying Central and South America in geography class this term, and Ms. Baker has used this study as the basis for a discussion of recent political events in a volatile Central American country. In addition to the usual lessons about the culture, resources, and products of the country, the students have learned about the distribution of land and income. The teacher has explained that a small percentage of the population controls a large part of the land and riches, exploiting the labor of most of the people and leaving them impoverished. She has compared government claims of constitutional rule with the reality of a military-dominated government that pursues genocidal policies against its own people, especially the native Indian population. In general, Ms. Baker has been very critical of the government, and she has praised those who oppose it. In answer to students' questions about our country's relations with this military-dominated government, she has explained in what ways the United States' policy in Central America is wrong.

Ms. Baker's geography lessons have made for interesting dinner table conversation, and some of the parents have become very angry about her schoolroom activities, particularly Russell Dent, a veteran of the armed forces and a conservative in his political orientation. According to Mr. Dent, Ms. Baker is not teaching. Rather, she has been indoctrinating the students to her point of view, an amalgam of left-wing values and a Marxist political position. She has distorted facts and has presented propaganda as instruction in geography. In doing so, she has abused her authority as a teacher and has violated the trust that the parents have placed in the school. As a teacher, Ms. Baker is acting as a surrogate for the parents, and she has no business introducing children to opinions that are not acceptable in the home. Furthermore, her criticism of the United States government is unpatriotic and has no place in an American classroom. It is Mr. Dent's firm opinion that Ms. Baker should not be allowed to manipulate impressionable young children in this manner, and he has said so in an angry phone call to the principal of Whittier School.

Upon hearing this charge, Margaret Baker has stated that she is not interested in anyone's propaganda, not that of her own government nor any other. In her geography class she deals only with facts, and those opinions that she might express in the classroom are rooted solidly in fact. As a teacher, she hopes that her students will come to understand that some facts must necessarily lead to certain conclusions, and her class is a good place to start. If she feigned neutrality in this case, she would be dishonest and fail in her responsibility as a teacher. The history text rightly condemns the Nazis for their actions. Should she do otherwise? If she avoided these sorts of issues, her students would miss the opportunity to develop their own opinions and skills in critical thought, and that would be unpatriotic. Ms. Baker is determined to continue her approach to instruction until someone shows her the error of her ways.

What is involved in a "political" education? Are the lessons Ms. Baker teaches important for a political education? Has she addressed the political issues? Does she have the right to teach such lessons? Should she modify her methods and/or content? Should a teacher be political? Would a teacher following Mr. Dent's demands be acting apolitically? Is it possible to be apolitical?

Resource Allocation

Aerospace Technologies, an expanding aviation engineering and manufacturing firm in a depressed area, has purchased a mainframe computer and so is no longer in need of the system of microcomputers it had previously used. The company has offered to donate these computers to the several school districts in the area. Because of the large demand and limited number of machines, Aerospace Technologies has conditioned its offer by saying the computers will be allocated to each district that wants them based upon the number of students in the district. This, they have determined, is the fairest way to proceed.

The school board of Plainview, a town of 30,000 with a chronically high rate of unemployment because of major industrial plant closings, has begun deliberation about the offer of twenty computers Aeorspace Technologies has made to the district. Most of the board members, teachers, and other citizens of Plainview are very excited about the gift. There are only a few computers at the town's two high schools—Academic High and Voc-Tech High. Unfortunately, there has never been any really serious consideration of acquiring any more soon, because funds have been extremely tight since the plant closings. Aerospace Technologies' offer is seen as a great opportunity for Plainview's children to catch up to the future.

There are many complications to consider before a decision on acceptance can be made, however. Introduction of a regular computer program would require funds for setting up a computer laboratory and hiring an instructor. But the board is barely operating in the black. Another school levy had been defeated the year before, forcing the postponement of planned textbook purchases, and the taxpayers are not amenable to a tax increase now, either. If they were to accept the computers, the board would have to cut back on academic or extracurricular programs.

Moreover, judging from the student response to the prospect of computer classes, twenty computers would barely satisfy the minimum needs of either of the two high schools if a decent computer course were to be instituted. Each school has a good claim to the need for computers. Academic High needs them to prepare students adequately for acceptance into colleges with first-rate engineering and science programs. Teachers and parents from that school argue that our country needs scientists and engineers to keep it strong. It would be a shame if talented students interested in entering those fields were lost to the nation because educational opportunities were lacking. (Incidentally, it was generally acknowledged that the representative of Aerospace Technologies, while expressing no directives about where the computers should go, did indicate that his company, which was constantly in need of new engineers, would be particularly pleased if the computers found their way into schools emphasizing college-prep courses.) And though some of the parents of Academic students could, and have, bought home computers, many other parents cannot afford to buy them. It will be these disadvantaged students who suffer most from lack of computers at the school.

The arguments of those teachers and parents from Voc-Tech High are different but still compelling. Computers are needed there, they say, in order to train programmers and computer-repair personnel. So much of local business has converted to computerized billing and inventory that there is a shortage of skilled people to handle programming and maintenance. Aerospace Technologies' offer presents one of the best opportunities for the children of working-class parents, who tend to go to Voc-Tech, to find high-status jobs in a promising new field. Their families cannot afford to buy home computers either. Many are still unemployed.

There is a third group that believes the offer should not be accepted. Several arguments are suggested. Some point out that Plainview graduates have, by and large, done very well without computer training. They accuse their opponents of using the "gift" as a way to raise taxes. Others say that any cutback in programs, which would certainly be required if the computers were to be used, would be unacceptable, considering how programs have been pared to a minimum already. They accuse their opponents of having misplaced priorities.

The board has asked the teachers, parents, and students from the town to bring arguments before it as to what should be done.

What would you say if you had to represent the position of the Academic High group? The Voc-Tech group? The antiacceptance group? If you were a board member, what would you recommend?

College or Workforce?

Central High School is the sole secondary school for Iron City, an aging northeastern industrial town. Iron City has seen better days and suffers from many of the problems that afflict our older towns, but Central High School has continued to serve the townspeople in the face of changing economics, demographics, and vocational aspirations.

Two facts about Iron City's population are important for any analysis of the school's place in the life of the town. Some residents of Iron City, Irish and Polish workers who have been in the mills and shops for generations, have great hope for their children. They want them to make a better life by attending college and escaping the mills. In recent years, their wishes on the subject have been reflected in an increased commitment to academic counseling and college-preparatory courses at Central High School.

Another group has had great impact on the town and the school. During the last twenty years large numbers of Latin Americans have arrived in Iron City, and their presence has affected the cultural life of the town and the educational mission of the schools. Central High School has sought to ease the process of assimilation for this group by emphasizing language instruction and instituting courses in cultural history. Yet, in the great melting pot, some things do remain the same. These Hispanic students now hold places in vocational education classes that formerly had been filled by first-generation Irish and Polish youngsters.

John O'Malley, the principal of Central High School, has been satisfied with this state of affairs. He feels that the school provides an adequate, sometimes excellent, education for its students and serves the town in a suitable manner. The curriculum is balanced in such a way that it allows each student to pursue individual needs and interests, and the guidance department takes an active role in the process of selection. The rising numbers of graduates who attend college has been a source of pride for Mr. O'Malley.

Given these perceptions, it is not surprising that Mr. O'Malley has had some difficulty understanding the complaints of Mrs. Virginia Cruz, the mother of a sophomore student at the school. According to Mrs. Cruz, her son, Dennis, has been treated unfairly by his guidance counselor. Dennis Cruz intends to continue his education after high school and wishes to register for college-preparatory courses. However, his adviser, Mrs. Kowolsky, does not think he will do well in these courses and has recommended that he register for the vocational-education program instead. In Mrs. Cruz's opinion, the adviser has no right to turn Dennis away from his dreams at such an early age, when many other students are given a fair chance. In fact, she feels that this is an example of Mrs. Kowolsky's prejudice. Mrs. Cruz has observed that a disproportionate number of Hispanic students are enrolled in vocational-education courses at Central High School, and more often than not, they are advised to apply for apprenticeships or join the armed forces upon graduation, rather than to apply for college admission. Mrs. Cruz believes that these practices should cease, for they are implicitly racist and discouraging to her son. He should receive the same sort of education and encouragement as other students. She will pursue this matter in a more assertive manner, unless her son's wishes are acknowledged.

Mr. O'Malley requested a conference with Mrs. Kowolsky, the head of the guidance department, in order to discuss this question. She has informed him that her decision is not a matter of prejudice at all. Rather, her recommendations are the result of a realistic and objective evaluation of the student's chances for academic and vocational success. Dennis Cruz has not been a top student, and his grades and test scores support this conclusion. Like many Hispanic students, he does not possess the language skills and cultural background that would enable him to do well in college. In Mrs. Kowolsky's opinion, she would be remiss in her responsibility as an educator to say or do otherwise. Furthermore, the financial burdens of higher education would be too great for the parents to bear. It would be unfair to recommend any other course of action and leave Dennis Cruz unprepared for those situations he will have to face in the workaday world. Besides, the existing system has been the path to success for other immigrant groups, and it is probably the best to pursue at this time.

Is equality of educational opportunity being denied Dennis? Are there functionalist arguments to support Mrs. Kowolsky? Is this a case of discrimination or sensible professional judgment?

Individual Differences and Equal Opportunity

A: In this land of opportunity, I believe that people, through the agency of education, should be free to grow and develop to the limits of their potential. After all, promoting the good of the individual ultimately serves the good of the society as a whole, doesn't it? Therefore, our schools must find ways to identify and develop the special talents of each student. We should not waste effort trying to make all people all things. It's not only inefficient but unfair to force someone without talent, without musical or scientific talent, for instance, to struggle and compete with those who have a gift in those areas. Would it not be more humane, as well as a greater benefit to society as a whole, to spare the untalented musician or the nonscientifically minded person from required courses in those areas? Let each learn what he is best suited for.

B: You make a good case, but I think it is wrongheaded. How can we decide what people are "best suited for"? It is morally wrong to ascribe characteristics to people. We have to permit people to demonstrate their talents. That can happen only if we give a broad, rich, and full education to all people. We should allow specialization and development of individual talent to proceed only partially in higher education, but most fully in private business, industry, or professional schools. Equal opportunity requires that.

A: Look who's trying to ascribe characteristics! You treat people as if they're all alike, as if you can bestow upon them everything they should need or be interested in. The point of equal opportunity is to provide an education that will develop everyone's individual talents. We have sophisticated tests that can identify human potential of all kinds. While general intelligence tests are our best indicators, we can also distinguish artistic and scientific talent, manual and intellectual skill; we can even test for personality factors that match different personality profiles to potential for success in suitable vocations. Our ability to screen and sort people gets more reliable each year as test makers create and sharpen their diagnostic instruments.

B: But if they are only getting better, are our tests really so good that we can use them to sort out human beings as if they were sheep? Even one mismatch or denial of opportunity for a person to grow in one direction rather than another would be a moral transgression against an individual that might change a whole life. If we can't be absolutely certain, then we shouldn't sort or track students at all. Even if tests were a hundred percent reliable, why should they be the criteria for deciding a person's future? Are we so sure that our standards are the right ones? Even reading groups in elementary school are question-able. We label children, and they tend to live up to our expectations, high or low. This could be a self-fulfilling prophecy. We stigmatize those we label as low achievers, and they do not get a fair chance to exceed our expectations. Opportunity means keeping open as many possibilities as possible for each and every student and not closing any.

A: While you're warmhearted, it is unfortunate that you are also mis-taken. Opportunity means giving everyone a chance to show poten-tial. But it is we who must measure that potential fairly and put people where they belong, where they will do themselves and society the most good. Why would we have schools if we didn't think children need guidance? It may be difficult, and our methods may be imper-fect, but specialized education is the only intelligent, efficient, and fair way to do things in a complex society like ours. Maybe a little general education is needed, but the special talents of individuals are the valuable common property of society. We are morally obligated to identify and train these unique capacities for the benefit of all.

Who do you think is right, *A* or *B*? Can equality of opportunity and individual differences ever be resolved? Do you think testing and special-ized schooling are functional or dysfunctional?

Social Reproduction

A: Every society has to reproduce itself; that is, initiate the young into its ways of life and its economic forms of distribution of goods and services. There may be arguments about how best to do this, but there doesn't seem to be much doubt about the necessity of doing this if a society is to continue its existence. Schools have an obligation to help in this, for the good of both society and individuals.

B: I think you're right, but I've been doing some serious thinking, and I've come to the conclusion that there is something wrong with certain "reproductive" practices in our school system. We think that it is designed to educate individuals, thereby giving them the skills and knowledge they will need in order to live full and productive lives as rational, autonomous agents in our society. But what do we actually do to the students in the institutional setting of an ordinary school like ours? We train them to accept unquestioningly life in a mindless bureaucracy, that dominant form of institutional life in our society. We blunt their creativity, individuality, and interest in learning by lock-stepping them through a system designed for monotonous mass production. We encourage competition, discourage the cooperative use of knowledge, and stress the selfish possession of it. The students repeat what we tell them, and the measure of success is a grade that can be "banked."

In these and many other ways, we teachers are immoral functionaries who mindlessly perpetuate the evils of our society and shape the next generation to fit into it. We are the unwitting tools of the ruling class, harnessed to work at their machines—the schools—whose products are docile workers and senseless, self-gratifying consumers. Sure, social reproduction is necessary; it is necessary to keep the ruling class in power!

A: Your rhetoric shocks me, but you just may be right. If you are, we certainly do some morally questionable things to students in the name of education. You make it sound more like indoctrination or conditioning than education. However, I'm not sure that your argument holds water.

How is it possible for a society to exist without socializing the young into it? How can it be morally wrong to do this when it is the only possible thing to do? Who is this "ruling class" that you're talking about, anyway? Big business? Politicians? Intellectuals? The rich? How do they control and use public schools in furthering their interests? I always thought that ordinary citizens serving on boards of education and professional educators—certainly not rich people—controlled things in the schools. They certainly don't intend to accomplish evil or exploit the children. Maybe most of us encourage competition, but what's wrong with that? Without it there would be no sports in the world, let alone business, and it provides a valuable lesson about the effort needed to make a living. Life is competitive.

Moreover, in our schools we teachers do try to develop our students' ability to think. If you can think, you can question and even change the system. So, if teachers teach children to think critically, they are doing something important, not questionable, aren't they? Besides, I'm not sure that I understand where you stand. Are you more concerned with facts or ideology? You make education sound like a conspiracy, but I think that most teachers genuinely try to empower their students to become the most that they can be in our society.

B: I'm not saying teachers are always aware of the consequences of their teaching; still, by means of our institutionalized, dehumanizing practices, we mold children into docile workers, television addicts, and mindless functionaries who only play at the kind of critical thinking we teach them. They talk politics over the bar or barbecue, but they don't make waves where it matters, on the job or in their dealings with bureaucracy. We train them to be that way. And that's the most they can become in our society because that's the way our schools are.

Who do you think is right, *A* or *B*? What do schools reproduce?

Equal but Separate

Deerpark School of Sylvan is part of the new Madison County Consolidated School District, a planned realignment of educational facilities and government. The new system combines, under a central county administration, the old schools of Jefferson City, which have been dominated by minorities and the urban poor in recent years, with the modern schools of the richer suburbs. This plan was developed as a result of pressure from Jefferson City residents and federal attorneys in order to guarantee educational parity and an acceptable racial balance in the area schools. It also provides additional revenue and improved services for the city schools. Under this plan, many students from Jefferson City now attend schools in surrounding towns like Sylvan.

Some teachers have followed these students to their new schools, as part of a limited reassignment of faculty in the new county system. Rosemary Andrews, a fourth-grade instructor, is among this group. Rosemary had come to Jefferson City with the Teachers Corps ten years ago, and she had remained with the city school system afterwards. Her years in these schools had been full of struggle and happiness. She and her fellows had worked hard to provide a decent education for disadvantaged children, using meager resources, determination, and imagination. Rosemary was a bit sad that a period of educational experimentation in Jefferson City had ended, but she believed that the new system would be best for the students in the long run. Her decision to transfer to Deerpark School was based, in part, upon a desire to follow the progress of the Jefferson City children in the new program.

Upon arriving in her new classroom on the first day of school, Rosemary discovered that she has followed these children much more closely than she had expected. Most of the children in her classroom are from Jefferson City. After consultation with another teacher, Rosemary found that all of the students in the other fourth-grade class are from the Sylvan area. In her opinion, this state of affairs does not accord with the spirit and intent of the agreement that created the unified county school district. The present arrangement at Deerpark School will only perpetuate de facto racial and economic segregation and minimize the desirable educational objectives that the consolidation plan was designed to encourage. The children in this classroom will have little personal contact with the other students and will remain strangers, possibly antagonists, to the children of Sylvan. Deerpark School seems to have abandoned any official responsibility to direct the racial and cultural interaction that might ameliorate the cleavages afflicting life in Madison County. This will only serve to harm the interests of both groups of children. In a very real sense, the school is an educational failure. It is undemocratic in its practices, and it is not really desegregated. Rosemary Andrews decided to confront the principal on this matter.

Robert Shire, the principal of Deerpark School and a resident of Sylvan, attempted to assuage Rosemary's anger and explained the present placement policy at the school. Deerpark School and the people of Sylvan will comply with the provisions of the consolidation plan, but they also intend to preserve the educational quality of the school. Over the years, Deerpark School has developed a very progressive, unified curriculum and has been very successful in its educational mission. The Jefferson City children will need time to adjust to the new curriculum. Also, the students from the city are not as educationally advanced as their new peers, and the standardized test scores for reading and mathematics show this. It will take time to bring their performance up to the proper grade level. Under these circumstances, Mr. Shire believes that it would be disruptive to instruction and unfair to both groups of children if they were thrown together with no regard for educational attainments. Mr. Shire asked Rosemary to have patience with the present situation.

Consider this case from a conflict theorist's viewpoint. How did the predesegregation situation manifest the interests of the dominant class? Does Mr. Shire represent that interest? Does Rosemary? Would a conflict theorist consider desegregation to be an answer to educational inequality? In what ways would a functionalist's analysis of this case be different? What would you do if you were Rosemary?

Education for Work

A: One of the best preparations for the world of work is a good liberal arts education. The personnel director of any major business will tell you that he looks for bright undergraduates without worrying about their specific majors, just as long as they've gotten good grades. Liberal arts majors learn to think and articulate ideas and that's just what business needs.

B: I'm not so sure that four years of college are necessary to learn to think and be an articulate person. I think that having a college education is just one more screening device and one more social-class barrier skewing opportunities for good jobs toward those who can afford college. Besides, don't policemen need to be able to think? We ordinarily don't require them to have college degrees, do we?

A: Well, no, but people in high-level managerial jobs need to be sophisticated and cultured, need to be able to meet and mix with the right people, and those are things made possible by a good liberal college education.

B: Just as I said, a college education is not learning the necessary knowledge for a higher-level job; it's learning the trappings of the upper classes.

A: No, it's not like that. It's learning about humanistic things like Shakespeare and great art and music, things that develop a person as a human being and make life richer, not in a material sense, but humanistically.

B: Well, if that's true, then why don't we give everybody a liberal education? Why do some get tracked into vocational-technical education? And wouldn't our police forces be better if they were more humane? Why not require a liberal education for policemen?

How would a conflict theorist view a liberal education? How would a functionalist? Is a liberal education the best education for all?

Workforce School

Maria Ortega's first teaching job was at Elmo High, an inner-city school in a deteriorating neighborhood with a high rate of drug abuse and crime. Whenever she told friends where she worked, they were shocked, felt sorry for her, and some even said they'd rather not teach than have to take a job in a place like that. "But someone has to teach there," Maria would always reply. How else could the culturally and economically deprived students at Elmo have a chance to get out of the ghetto like she did?

When Maria had begun at Elmo, it had been just like many other inner-city schools: a high drop-out rate, drug and discipline problems, a staff with low morale, and students who saw school work as irrelevant to their lives. But then Hector Gomez became principal. He was given a free hand to develop an experimental curriculum by the Board of Education, and things really changed.

Maria was a second-year teacher at Elmo when Mr. Gomez arrived, and she, like the rest of the faculty, was caught up in the spirit of his enterprise to change the school and make a difference in the lives of the students. That was five years ago, and now Maria was reflecting on how much had changed since then.

The local police were seldom called now to break up gang fights or investigate thefts. The school corridors were clean, and the passings between classes orderly. Attendance was high; so was the morale of the staff. It didn't seem possible that all this was due to Mr. Gomez's charismatic personality and his decision to make the school a vocational-work-study, community-cooperative school. Mr. Gomez visited local businesses and small factories and signed them up to accept as "interns" students on released work-study assignments. Teachers eagerly took turns visiting students at work sites and finding ways to bring the world of work meaningfully into the classes they taught at Elmo. After they graduated, many students were finding jobs in places where they had interned. It seemed like a miracle to Maria!

Then one day a group of students came in to see her at the end of the day. Their spokesperson said, "Mrs. Ortega, can we apply to college with our curriculum at Elmo and become teachers like you? Our guidance counselor told us we don't have enough academic credits."

Have Mr. Gomez's changes provided real opportunities for the students or simply fit them into the system? Would the belated addition of optional academic credit courses change the situation significantly?

Class Bias?

Marilyn Todd, a veteran teacher with more than twenty-five years' experience, currently teaches English in the junior high school of a small town of very rich and very poor residents. She is considered a fine teacher and has been responsible for the excellent training of hundreds of young people who come from the best families. Over the years, her seniority has given her the right to avoid poorer students (in both senses of the term) and teach only the seventh- and eighth-grade accelerated sections. The two regular sections of heterogeneously grouped seventh-graders are taught English by Sarah Gold, the general music teacher, and Dominic Quattrone, the art teacher, who have been employed at the school five and four years respectively on a part-time, mixed-assignment basis. Marilyn Todd has been a big help to them in their teaching of their sole English class, and they are grateful for her assistance. However, a certain trend is becoming evident, and the two younger teachers are disturbed about Ms. Todd.

At the end of every year, seventh-grade faculty meet to determine class placement for the next year's eighth graders. Anyone who feels strongly that a student should be moved from the heterogeneous "average" class to an homogeneous "accelerated" class (or vice versa) makes the recommendation, discusses it with the other teachers, makes a final decision, and passes the assignment on to the principal. Parent input is also considered, and there have been cases in which parent requests have overridden teacher recommendations.

Comparing notes with one another, Dom and Sarah have come to the unhappy conclusion that every seventh-grade student from the poor side of town whom either of them has ever recommended to be placed in Marilyn's top eighth-grade accelerated class has fared poorly. These are students who far outshone their peers in the average class, maintained steady A averages, were bright and consistently on track in class discussions. When they got to Ms. Todd's class, however, it was surprising that they seldom earned higher than a C (especially surprising considering Marilyn's reputation as an easy grader in all her sections) and that they often had personality clashes with Ms. Todd. Upon reflection, Dom and Sarah remembered feeling real resistance from Marilyn to their proposals of moving these children into her upper-level classes. Sarah wonders if Marilyn might regard her colleagues' teaching as inferior to her own, thus believing that their students would not be prepared to work at the level she demands from her classes. Dom thinks she really treats the students from poorer homes differently, but he can't put his finger on just how.

The latest victim from the seventh grade was a student of Dom's who had so surpassed his classmates that Dom needed to provide extra and more difficult work to challenge him. When this child entered Ms. Todd's eighth grade, she told other teachers that she suspected him of being learning disabled because he was such a poor student. He barely passed her course. Dom and Sarah were astounded, resentful, and perplexed when this finally came to light.

They decided they had to approach Marilyn about their concerns. Although they tried to be diplomatic, Ms. Todd reacted vehemently. She stated flatly that she resented the insinuation that she held preconceived notions about any incoming student. All were judged on the same standards regardless of who they were. If any students did poorly, it was because they hadn't the ability to do the work or were unwilling to put in the effort to succeed.

If you were Dom or Sarah, how would you try to convince Marilyn that she was unconsciously biased? What, if anything, could you do as a teacher to safeguard against an unconscious class bias? Do you think this is a case of class bias, or could Marilyn be right?

Social Studies

John had been a social studies teacher at Humphrey High for twenty-five years. He had seen it change from a predominantly upwardly mobile, middle-class school to an ethnically imbalanced lower-class, non-achievement-oriented school. Students spoke very poor English, most could barely read, and discipline was always a problem. Still, John was able to maintain a rapport with his students, and he believed that above all they needed to understand the American way of life, appreciate our democratic political institutions, and see that opportunity was not closed to them if they were willing to work at making it.

The 1984 presidential campaign provided him with a real example that everyone knew about. For the first time in history, a woman ran as a vice-presidential candidate. What was more, she had come from immigrant parents, worked her way through college, become a teacher, studied law at night, become a public prosecutor, and been elected to Congress before being chosen to run. There was a lesson in all this hard work, education, and cumulative success for his students. John just had to find a way to get that lesson across.

If you were John, how would you try to teach that lesson? How would you answer the angry student who says, "It's like playing the lottery. With your 'American Dream' stories, you get everybody to work hard and contribute to society in the hope of getting a big payoff. But only a few win high places and good salaries, and in the meantime all our work keeps the system going for the benefit of the rich. Your 'lesson' is just a way to get more work out of us, and I'm not going to fall for it. Guarantee me a good-paying, white-collar job after graduation, and I'll think about it. You know you can't do that, so why should I work?"

Interpretation and Ethical Relativism

A: I can see that different groups of people have different ways of interpreting the same thing, but admitting that can lead to serious problems if you're not careful. For instance, it would be difficult to persuade anyone that you're right about something because they could always say, "That's just your interpretation." And what happens to our ethics if it's all just personal interpretations? If my ethical standards are taken to be my interpretation of right and wrong, how can I ever justify them to others? Whatever I do because I think it's right could be considered wrong according to someone else's interpretation.

B: I don't think an interpretivist viewpoint forces one to be that relativistic. Just because an interpretation is mine doesn't mean it can't be defended whenever it's challenged by someone else's. Some interpretations are better than others. You can influence someone to see the force behind different interpretations if you give compelling reasons.

A: But there's no reason why the other person should be compelled. In a case where we have a strong personal belief, we have to act on that belief regardless of what the other person says. Morality requires that, doesn't it? Suppose you visit a society that practices child sacrifice as part of its religious ceremonies. They would consider it right. What right would you have to tell them it's wrong?

B: I'd have every right. The interpretivist isn't forced to condone others' actions. He's forced to understand their actions from *their* point of view, not just his. He might see that those people were not bloodthirsty savages, but rather thoughtful and religious. He might find that the children in that society are more esteemed than in supposedly humane societies that allow millions of children to starve and live in poverty. With an understanding of the people, he would be better able to explain his views to them, and he'd have the right to assert the applicability of his values to their society. We *can* criticize others' interpretations. The point is *not* to do it without understanding them.

A: Well, if that's all we can do, it's not worth much. While you would be there haggling over interpretations, how many children would you allow to be killed? How could an interpretivist position justify you in *doing* something about it rather than just talking about it?

Do you think ethics is relative to society? Can an interpretivist hold ethical standards? What do you believe about right and wrong? As a teacher, are there any behaviors of students you would deem ethically unacceptable? On what grounds?

The New Student

Anastasos Kostos began the year as a new student in the sixth grade at Walden School. His father was sent to the United States by his company to observe the new automation in the plant in Middletown. Ms. Nichols was delighted to have a foreign student in her class, even if he couldn't stay the full year. She felt that her students could learn a lot about the world outside of Middletown in ways neither she nor her books could teach them.

Anastasos was a double delight. He was very bright and articulate. He was polite and pleasant. And he was always willing to share examples from his culture with the class whenever Ms. Nichols called on him to do so. He never got into trouble and always acted kindly toward his fellow students. Then why, Ms. Nichols wondered, was he so obviously shunned by his classmates? Why hadn't even one become his friend? She was genuinely puzzled.

She tried to think of what was going on in the minds of her students. Did they share an unwritten rule that seemed to be part and parcel of small-town Middletown's culture: "Beware of outsiders, especially foreigners; they aren't like us"? Did they resent, perhaps even without knowing it, the attention she was giving Anastasos and the positive ways she was greeting "weird" social practices?

Or might it be something more visible? She remembered reading once that people from different cultures used different body language. She had seen children pull away from Anastasos when he stood very close to talk to them or when he touched them as he talked. Was that part of the "rules" of informal friendly conversation in his world and uncomfortable behavior according to the unspoken mores of Middletown, where proper distance showed respect and anything closer was too intimate or rude?

Ms. Nichols had a hunch it was Anastasos' "body language" that was the root of the trouble. But now she had another problem. Should she try to get Anastasos to change his "rules of friendly conversation" or change the class's? If she decided to change either, how could she do it?

Is there any solution to her problem? Are there other possible interpretations of how her students are perceiving Anastasos?

Mainstream or Not?

Dr. Case, principal of Pinebrook Elementary School, was disgusted as he hung up his phone. Phone calls to Mr. Morano, Anthony's father, to report his son's latest behavioral outburst, or failure to do his classwork, or a problem with another child had become almost a daily event. He sometimes wondered why he bothered to call this ineffectual parent, who seemed unable to handle the boy. Yet he was the only parent the child had; his mother had abandoned the family and was presently in a drug rehabilitation program, and didn't someone have to be responsible for the boy?

The complaints of Anthony's classroom teachers had increased over the years as he had grown older. His behavior had become increasingly deviant. In addition to doing little classwork or schoolwork, he fought with other children, stole toys and money, destroyed school property, and was a general disruption to the learning process in the classroom. Dr. Case was well aware of Anthony's background. He had spent many hours hearing and reading the reports of Anthony's caseworker, psychologist, special education teacher, and parent advocate, among others. Dr. Case attended meetings of the Committee on the Handicapped, which had labeled Anthony emotionally handicapped.

Mr. Rainer, Anthony's special education teacher, asked that Dr. Case and his staff give Anthony greater support. The school district had made a commitment to mainstream as many of its learning disabled and emotionally handicapped students as possible. Anthony did spend two hours each day in the special education resource room with Mr. Rainer. Despite his poor home background, he was reading at grade level and scored at grade level on reading and math achievement tests. Tests of IQ indicated he had above average ability. He was an alert, attractive child, who seemed to enjoy school and was learning. Mr. Rainer reminded Dr. Case that every child had a right to the best education possible.

Dr. Case was well aware of the law protecting handicapped students. He could also see the problem from the larger perspective of preparing each child to be a productive member of society in the future. Mrs. Black, Anthony's classroom teacher, however, was distraught and shared her concerns with Dr. Case. Anthony did little work in her class. He disrupted her lessons and bothered the children who sat near him. She suspected he was the culprit who had been taking the children's lunch money and belongings. He seemed to enjoy confrontation with his classmates and teacher. Perhaps that was why he told Mr. Rainer he liked school. Mrs. Black often had to send Anthony to the office. There he caused problems, too. He rarely sat quietly, as he was supposed to do. Rather, he asked questions about incoming phone calls, wandered about, and had conversations with parents and others who entered the school office.

Mr. Morano, Anthony's father, asked that the school be understanding. He believed that despite Anthony's emotional problems, he was receiving a fine education and that his behavior was improving. Anthony's caseworker supported the parent. She had been with the family since Anthony's early childhood and saw great improvement in his development. The school, she said, had a responsibility to this child, as to every child, and shouldn't turn its back on him.

Dr. Case's dilemma was a complex one. As an educator and school leader, where did his responsibility lie? Should he insist that Anthony be sent to a special school, thereby removing the problems he caused and the many complaints from staff, students, and parents? Or did the school have a responsibility to educate this child, who was learning despite his behavioral problems? Sometimes, Dr. Case felt the new laws protecting handicapped students were slowing the process of education. On the other hand, he could see the larger societal implications of this legislation.

If you were an interpretivist, how would you analyze this case? How would your analysis differ from that of a Marxist? A functionalist? What would you recommend for Anthony if you were Dr. Case?

Social Conditioning and Freedom

A: The two most powerful influences on children as they are growing up are the home and the school. Both present children with the only view of the world they will have until they are adults and then, only maybe, will they come to see other ways of interpreting "reality." Most will not, of course. Unfortunately for our children, it is not *a* view of the world they feel they are getting; it is the only world there is for them because they are totally dependent on those who teach them. This total "indoctrination" makes them prisoners of their culture and often of their class. We say we educate for freedom and autonomy, but basically, that's impossible.

B: Freedom is only impossible if you hold an impossible view of it. No one can be free from family and school, language and culture. We all need such experiences to become persons. There is no uncontaminated place free from these things for acquiring freedom. Freedom is earned by questioning things you were taught unquestioningly. It is developing standards of judgment and integrity that allow you to responsibly accept or reject views and norms, beliefs and values, that your home, school, or culture passed on to you. An individual's life in society is inheritance, participation, and contribution, and one's contribution takes the form of critical reflection and action on what you and society are or might become.

A: You sound very idealistic. Isn't it true that part of what we learn at home and school are tacit rules and norms that not only govern what we feel is basically right or wrong in human conduct but also define methods of being critical and thinking independently? Aren't even norms of rationality passed on, inherited by the next generation, and participated in in different cultures? A "possible" view of freedom can't be based on rationality and integrity with regard to personal standards. There are no such things. There are only socially derived practices and beliefs and ways of thinking.

B: Of course, our social world is a shared world. How impossible it would be if we each had to "reinvent the wheel," discover for ourselves without help those useful ways of doing things and ways of thinking our society has developed through generations of individual contributions! My point is that we can do more than mindlessly play the games we've been taught by home and school. We can question, think, and act to change ourselves, and even to change society in some instances, and that is a freedom beyond the prison of social custom and culture. It may not be easy, but it's *possible* to rise above the teachings of others. Don't confuse the difficult with the impossible. Human freedom is not a gift, it's earned the hard way. It is part of the process of becoming an autonomous person.

A: You make it sound good, but don't you see what you're saying is just a reflection of the liberal Western political tradition you were raised in? You'd believe very different things if you were born and schooled in a country with a different political tradition.

B: You might be right, but I still believe that it would be possible, for either this me or that me you invented, to question and alter my basic beliefs about freedom.

A: You might be right, but all this is so hypothetical; we'll never know the answer. So why bother then? What difference will continuing our argument make to us, or anyone else for that matter? Either we are or aren't free and our arguments won't change that.

B: Oh, yes, they will; just try acting freely when you don't believe it's possible.

Do you think freedom is possible? Can one be critical of one's culture and its "legitmate" ways of making knowledge claims? Does education provide a cultural prison or a launching pad for freedom?

Interpretation and Epistemic Relativism

A: Functionalists and neo-Marxists have to realize that they just see the same things differently and that neither has *the* Truth of the matter. Each group of scholars, just like each religious, ethnic, or even national group, has their "way" of seeing the world and interpreting what's happening in it. We have to realize that that's the way it is and that to look for one "right" view is inappropriate.

B: Do you mean there is no true description of the relationship between school and society? If that's so, then you can't claim to have the correct way to look at schooling or educational research either.

A: Yes, I can. Look, it's like observing three people who are wearing three differently tinted sunglasses. One says the world looks gray; another, brown; and the third, pink. They're all right in one sense, but the world isn't all gray, brown, or pink. I can look through their glasses and see what they see, but I know when I'm wearing glasses, and they don't.

B: That's a pretty persuasive analogy, but isn't there a sense in which everybody has to be wearing glasses, that is, using *some* interpretive framework, to view the world or other people's interpretation of it?

A: Yes, but don't you see the difference between *knowing* that's what everyone must be doing and doing it unknowingly while claiming what you see is the only true view?

B: I think so, but doesn't that force you to say nobody's interpretation can be better than anybody else's? After all, seeing the world pink isn't getting a better or worse view of it than seeing it gray or brown. We pick the sunglasses that most appeal to us for personal subjective reasons and not because one gives us a clearer image of the world.

A: You're pushing my analogy a bit hard, but I'd like to think there are better or worse interpretations. Some fit the facts better, and some accommodate new facts better, and some fail to fit in things that seem intuitively important.

B: But aren't what count as "facts" determined by one's interpretative framework?

A: The answer is hermeneutics.

What do you think? Are some interpretations better than others? Can an interpretivist make legitimate knowledge claims?

A Third-World School System

Kote Kopella returned to his country after five years of doctoral study in education in the United States. His country hadn't changed much. Twenty-five years after achieving independence from colonial rule, it was still politically unstable. Agriculture was still the mainstay of the population, both for its own subsistence and for exports needed to produce income to buy needed technical products. The dream of the national planners was to create a workforce through education that would use the raw materials of the country to produce nonagricultural products for export and give the people the opportunity to leave the harsh work on the farms for the more pleasant working and material conditions of urban industrial society.

Chosen as one of the future leaders and builders of the national educational system that would fulfill these important purposes, Kote was sent abroad to study. But as a student in the United States he had learned about functionalist, Marxist, and interpretivist views of schooling, and he was confused. If only he had just learned about one view, he could have gone back home and set to work with others to help plan the national educational system without the problem of mixed perspectives that he now had. From the point of view of the Marxists, he could see that a sharp division of classes was growing in his country, as the rich few who were in good positions at independence used their power to maintain themselves. Sure, they offered schooling to the masses of illiterates from the farms, but just enough to make them able workers in the factories and not enough to become the owners. From the point of view of the functionalists, he could see the need for a school system that could help select and train the talent needed in a new society that was emerging from near primitive forms of agriculture into an era of industrialization and economic growth in which all the population could share in better food, housing, health, and material comfort. Bribery and family friends should not get incompetent people into managerial positions; the only criterion should be proven competence. From the point of view of the interpretivists, Kote could see the need to find ways in the schools to maintain the many good things about tribal and agricultural life that fostered a sense of community, a feeling of well-being, and a satisfaction with life that had flourished in his country even under colonial rule. To maintain their integrity in a rapidly changing world, his people needed to preserve and pass on their ways of life.

If you were Kote, what sorts of proposals would you make for your nation's school system? Can the insights from these differing views be made compatible in practice?

The Curriculum

A: The basic curriculum in our elementary and secondary schools provides the general skills and knowledge required for all persons to become participants and sharers in a common social world.

B: What common social world? There are the rich and the poor, the powerful and the weak, the privileged and the rest of us. We learn our place in school, and the unfairness of our social world is preserved and legitimated by the system. The curriculum develops false consciousness.

C: No, *A* is right. The basic curriculum, both overt and hidden, serves to prepare people to function effectively in society, and that provides them with an opportunity to succeed in life. You can't do that if you can't read or write, and you can't even make people aware of their so-called false consciousness unless they've been educated. The curriculum prepares people for the complex technical world they will have to live and work in. Schools develop the skills and attitudes needed for productive employment in our businesses and industries, which, in turn, provide the goods and services necessary to maintain the high standards of living we all desire. In these ways, schools provide equality of opportunity for material well-being and success in life to all members of society.

B: Then why does socioeconomic class origin correlate so highly with school achievement and occupational economic success? I'll tell you why; because while the schools falsely claim to offer opportunity, they really teach the underclass who they are and train them to be docile workers who accept a life of artificially created needs being filled by cheap products and forms of entertainment that also serve to fill pockets of the rich.

A: But neither of you has really spoken to the curriculum. What it actually is appears to get lost in your political rhetoric. Isn't the curriculum just a distillation of the formal knowledge system of our culture? Don't we learn in school how to be full participants in our shared social world?

B: On the surface, yes, but the *real* curriculum is hidden, and it reproduces and legitimates the class structure.

C: Some of the curriculum is "hidden," certainly, though now we can see it better because of our research. We do teach norms and attitudes that are important for succeeding in our democratic society. What's wrong with that? What's wrong with learning independence, achievement, specificity, and universalism? It makes for better people and a better society. A is also right; the subjects learned in school are distillations of the knowledge systems we share as a culture and so all should have some acquaintance with them.

A: We also share beliefs and norms, one of the most basic and important being that individual persons are autonomous. I believe that we must teach people what they need in order to be autonomous participants in our society. That means that the curriculum, both manifest and latent, should provide a core of the intersubjectively shared knowledge that constitutes our culture and social ways. It also should help students to see that that's what social life is and that we all have a hand in making it what it is. Finally, students should see that only by being a participating member of some social system can we seek to fulfill our individual needs and purposes as human beings.

B: Individual needs and purposes are defined by class consciousness!

C: No, they are defined in a social context of progress. *A* lacks a human political perspective, and that's why his theory seems groundless. At least *B* and I have political theories of the curriculum even though we don't agree about them. *A* must be naive not to think of the curriculum in political terms. The curriculum can't be apolitical.

With which view of the curriculum do you feel more comfortable? Why? Can the curriculum be apolitical?

NOTES
ANNOTATED BIBLIOGRAPHY
INDEX

Notes

Chapter 2

1. For a fuller treatment of functionalism, see Robert K. Merton, *Social Theory and Social Structure, Revised* (New York: Free Press, 1967), pp. 19–84; and Wilbert E. Moore, "Functionalism," in *A History of Sociological Analysis*, ed. T. B. Bottommore and L. R. Nisbet (New York: Basic Books, 1978). Also useful is Anthony Giddens, *Studies in Social and Political Theory* (New York: Basic Books, 1977), pp. 96–134.

2. Moore, "Functionalism," p. 355.

3. See Talcott Parsons, "Evolutionary Universals in Society," *American Sociological Review* 29 (June 1964): 339–57.

4. Robert Dreeben, *On What Is Learned in School* (Reading, Mass.: Addison-Wesley, 1968), p. 5.

5. See *ibid.*, pp. 66–84.

6. *Ibid.*, p. 93.

7. Philip W. Jackson, *Life in Classrooms* (New York: Holt, Rinehart and Winston, 1968), pp. 1–38. While Jackson explicates the concept of hidden curriculum, he does not explicitly identify himself as a functionalist. In fact, we shall refer to his work again when we discuss the interpretivist approach. If the idea of "hidden curriculum" is intriguing to you at this point, however, you might pause to consider the case by that name in chapter 8.

8. See Theodore W. Schultz, *The Economic Value of Education* (New York: Columbia University Press, 1963), pp. 1–20.

Chapter 3

1. There is a fourth explanation, which we will not deal with here. John Ogbu *(The Next Generation* [New York: Academic Press, 1974], p. 7) identifies it as the failure of the traditional school to provide the appropriate kind of learning environment for minority children. Alternative schools, open education, performance contracting, and so forth are the sorts of reforms urged to rectify this perceived dysfunctioning of schools.

2. Richard Herrnstein and Charles Murray, *The Bell Curve: Intelligence and Class Structure in American Life* (New York: The Free Press, 1994).

3. For a more detailed development of Banfield's views than are sketched here, see Edward Banfield, *The Unheavenly City: The Nature and Future of Our Urban Crisis* (Boston: Little Brown, 1970).

4. *Ibid.*, pp. 23–24.

5. Daniel Patrick Moynihan, "Employment, Income, and the Ordeal of the Negro Family," in *The Negro in America*, ed. Talcott Parsons and Kenneth B. Clark (Boston: Beacon Press, 1967), pp. 134–59.

6. Robert K. Merton, *Social Theory and Social Structure* (New York: Free Press, 1967), p. 29.

7. *Ibid.*, p. 32, emphasis in original.

8. *Ibid.*, p. 35.

9. *Ibid.*, p. 51.

10. Anthony Giddens, *Studies in Social and Political Theory* (New York: Basic Books, 1977), p. 108.

11. See Arthur Stinchcombe, *Constructing Social Theories* (New York: Harcourt, Brace and World, 1968).

12. For an elaboration of this criticism, see Giddens, *Studies in Social and Political Theory*, p. 110.

13. *Ibid.*, p. 110.

Chapter 4

1. Randall Collins, "Functional and Conflict Theories of Educational Stratification," in *Power and Ideology in Education*, ed. Jerome Karabel and A. H. Halsey (New York: Oxford University Press, 1977), p. 121.

2. Harry Braverman, *Labor and Monopoly Capital* (New York: Monthly Review Press, 1974).

3. Collins, "Functional and Conflict Theories of Educational Stratification," p. 122.

4. Louis Althusser, *Lenin and Philosophy and Other Essays* (New York: New Left Books, 1971), pp. 123–73.

5. Samuel Bowles and Herbert Gintis, *Schooling in Capitalist America: Educational Reform and the Conditions of Economic Life* (New York: Basic Books, 1976), pp. 102–25.

6. *Ibid.*, p. 34.

Chapter 5

1. Jean Anyon, "Social Class and the Hidden Curriculum of Work," *Journal of Education* 162 (Winter 1980): 67–92.

2. *Ibid.*, p. 73.

3. *Ibid.*, p. 74.

4. *Ibid.*, p. 75.

5. *Ibid.*, p. 85.

6. For a general statement of McDermott's interactional perspective, see R. P. McDermott, "Social Relations as Contexts for Learning in School," in *Knowledge and Values in Social and Educational Research*, ed. Eric Bredo and Walter Feinberg (Philadelphia: Temple University Press, 1982), pp. 252–70.

7. Ray C. Rist, "Student Social Class and Teacher Expectation: The Self-Fulfilling Prophecy in Ghetto Education," *Harvard Educational Review* 40, no. 3 (August 1970): 441–51.

8. Pierre Bourdieu and Jean-Claude Passeron, *Reproduction in Education, Society, and Culture* (London: Sage, 1977).

9. See Pierre Bourdieu, "Cultural Reproduction and Social Reproduction," paper given at the British Sociological Association Conference, 1970; *idem*, "The Aristocracy of Culture," trans. Richard Nice, *Media Culture and Society* 23 (1980): 225–54.

10. For an elaboration of this point, see Eric Bredo and Walter Feinberg, "Meaning, Power and Pedagogy: Pierre Bourdieu and Jean-Claude Passeron, *Reproduction in Education, Society, and Culture*," *Journal of Curriculum Studies* 11, no. 4 (1979): 315–32.

11. Paul Willis, *Learning to Labor: How Working Class Kids Get Working Class Jobs* (New York: Columbia University Press, 1981), p. 1.

12. *Ibid.,* p. 22.

13. *Ibid.,* p. 64.

14. Anthony Giddens, *Studies in Social and Political Theory* (New York: Basic Books, 1977), p. 110.

15. David M. Halperin, *One Hundred Years of Homosexuality: And Other Essays on Greek Love,* New York: Routledge, p. 15–40.

16. C. G. Prado *Starting with Foucault: An Introduction to Genealogy,* Boulder: Westview Press, 1995, p. 88.

17. William E. Connolly, *Identity/Difference: Democratic Negotiations of Political Paradox,* Ithaca, NY: Cornell University Press, 1991, p. 94.

18. Michel Foucault, (ed.) *Herculine Barbin: Being the Recently Discovered Memoirs of a Nineteenth Century Hermaphrodite,* Brighton, England: Harvester Press, 1980.

19. Michel Foucault, *I, Pierre Rivière, Having Slaughtered My Mother, My Sister, and My Brother—A Case of Parricide in the 19th Century,* New York: Pantheon Books, 1975.

20. Michel Foucault, *The Order of Things: An Archaeology of the Human Sciences,* New York: Random House, 1970.

21. Michel Foucault, *Discipline and Punish: The Birth of The Prison,* New York: 1979.

22. Michel Foucault, *Herculine Barbin.*

23. Chris Mayo, *Disputing the Subject of Sex: Sexual Identity and School Controversy in New York State, 1986–1993.* Urbana: Unpublished doctoral dissertation, 1997.

24. Jaggar, A. *Feminist Politics and Human Nature,* Totowa, NJ: Rowman and Allanheld, 1983, p. 5.

25. Catharine MacKinnon, *Feminism Unmodified: Discourses on Life and Law,* Cambridge: Harvard University Press, 1987, p.37

26. Nancy Fraser, *Unruly Practices: Power, Discourse and Gender in Contemporary Social Theory,* Minneapolis: University of Minnesota Press, 1989, pp. 144–161.

27. Carol Gilligan, *In a Different Voice: Psychological Theory and Woman's Development,* Cambridge: Harvard University Press, 1982.

28. Nel Noddings, *Caring: A Feminist Approach to Ethics & Moral Education,* Berkeley: University of California Press, 1984.

Chapter 6

1. Sara Lawrence Lightfoot, *The Good High School: Portraits of Character and Culture* (New York: Basic Books, 1983).

2. Peter Winch, *The Idea of a Social Science and Its Relation to Philosophy* (London: Routledge and Kegan Paul, 1958), p. 83.

3. Clifford Geertz, *The Interpretation of Cultures* (New York: Basic Books, 1973), p. 6, emphasis in original.

4. Rom Harrè and Paul Secord, *The Explanation of Social Behaviour* (Totowa, N.J.: Littlefield, Adams, 1973).

5. R. P. McDermott and Lois Hood, "Institutional Psychology and the Ethnography of Schooling," in *Ethnography and Education: Children In and Out of School*, ed. Perry Gilmore and Alan Glatthorn (Washington, D.C.: Center for Applied Linguistics, 1982).

6. *Ibid.*, p. 240, emphasis in original.

7. *Ibid.*, p. 238.

8. R. P. McDermott, "Achieving School Failure: An Anthropological Approach to Illiteracy and Social Stratification," in *Education and Culture Process, ed.* George D. Spindler (New York: Holt, Rinehart and Winston, 1974).

Chapter 7

1. Philip W Jackson, *Life in Classrooms* (New York: Holt, Rinehart and Winston, 1968).

2. Philip A. Cusick, *Inside High School: The Student's World* (New York: Holt, Rinehart and Winston, 1973).

3. See Alan Peshkin, *Growing Up American* (Chicago: The University of Chicago Press, 1978); and *idem, The Imperfect Union* (Chicago: The University of Chicago Press, 1982).

4. For an interesting description of how we do many social things with words besides communicate propositional meaning, see J. L. Austin, *How to Do Things with Words* (New York: Oxford University Press, 1962); and John R. Searle, *Speech Acts* (Cambridge, England: Cambridge University Press, 1969).

5. Lyn Corno, "What It Means to Be Literate About Classrooms," in *Classroom and Literacy*, ed. David Bloom (Norwood, N.J.: Ablex Publishing Corp., 1989), p. 30.

6. Amy Gutman, *Democratic Education* (Princeton, N.J.: Princeton University Press, 1987).

7. *Ibid,* p. 39.

Annotated Bibliography

This list includes recent as well as older references that are either considered classics or offer the best introduction to the topic.

Adelman, Irma, and Morris, Cynthia Taft. *Economic Growth and Social Equity in Developing Countries*. Stanford, CA: Stanford University Press, 1973.

    Adelman and Morris reexamine and challenge some of the functionalist assumptions about the relationship between economic growth and democracy. Using data from a number of Third-World countries, they find that economic growth is often followed by a reduction in political and economic equality.

Apple, Michael. *Ideology and Curriculum* (2nd ed.). London: Routledge and Kegan Paul, 1990; and *Teachers and Texts: A Political Economy of Class and Gender Relations in Education*. New York: Routledge, Chapman and Hall, 1988.

    In these books, Apple explores issues of class, gender, power, and hegemony from a neo-Marxist perspective.

Baran, Paul, and Sweezy, Paul. *Monopoly Capital: An Essay on the American Economic and Social Order*. New York: Monthly Review Press, 1968.

    A Marxist analysis of the direction that capitalism has taken in recent times.

Berger, Peter L., and Luckmann, Thomas. *The Social Construction of Reality*. Middlesex, England: Penguin Books, 1972.

    A good general introduction to an interpretivist point of view and its description of socialization.

Bernstein, Richard J. *The Restructuring of Social and Political Theory*. Philadelphia: University of Pennsylvania Press, 1976.

    A detailed explication and criticism of four different views of social theory: empirical theory, language analysis, phenomenology, and critical theory. Bernstein argues that each has something important to offer to our understanding of the social world.

Bowles, Samuel, and Gintis, Herbert. *Schooling in Capitalist America: Educational Reform and the Conditions of Economic Life*. New York: Basic Books, 1976.

    A Marxist analysis of the structural limits on the role of schooling in the development of individual growth, equal opportunity, and the development of labor power. Bowles and Gintis explore how schools legitimize inequality.

Bredo, Eric, and Feinberg, Walter, eds. *Knowledge and Values in Social and Educational Research.* Philadelphia: Temple University Press, 1982.

>This anthology provides examples of the philosophies behind different educational research methodologies and their implications for our understanding of school achievement.

Butts, R. Freeman. "Public Education and Political Community." In *History, Education and Public Policy,* edited by Donald Warren. Berkeley, CA: McCutchan, 1978.

>Butts explores the role of the school in the development of a democratic citizenry.

Connolly, William E. *Identity/Difference: Democratic Negotiations of Political Paradox.* Ithaca, NY: Cornell University Press, 1991.

>Connolly applies many of Foucault's ideas to political science, and to the issues that are involved in shaping individual and collective identities.

Denzin, Norman K., and Lincoln, Yvonna S., eds. *Handbook of Qualitative Research,* Thousand Oaks, CA: Sage, 1994.

>This book examines methodological issues in qualitative research.

Dewey, John. *Democracy and Education.* New York: Macmillan, 1916.

>This is the classic progressive educator's statement of the social role of schooling in a democratic society and teaching for the development of intelligence and reflective thinking.

Eisner, Elliot W. *The Enlightened Eye: Qualitative Inquiry and the Enhancement of Educational Practice.* New York: Macmillan, 1991.

>Develops a model of qualitative inquiry, drawn from the concepts of connoisseurship and criticism found in the arts and humanities, that is aimed at providing insights into ways to improve practice.

Eisner, Elliot W., and Peshkin, Alan, eds. *Qualitative Inquiry in Education: The Continuing Debate.* New York: Teachers College Press, 1990.

>Treats issues of subjectivity and objectivity, generalizability, validity, ethics, and the potential uses of qualitative methodology in educational research and evaluation.

Erickson, Fred. "Qualitative Methods in Research on Teaching." In *Handbook of Research on Teaching* (3rd ed.), edited by Merlin C. Wittrock. New York: Macmillan, 1987.

>A clearly written, detailed description of the aspects of teaching that best can be examined by the qualitative approach.

Foucault, Michel. *The Order of Things: An Archaeology of the Human Sciences.* New York: Random House, 1970.

>Foucault explores the rules of formation of various sciences showing how different sciences in the same time period use the same rules to construct their object and to develop systems of classification. The study raises unsettling questions about the possibility of the growth of knowledge.

Foucault, Michel. *I, Pierre Rivière Having Slaughtered My Mother, My Sister, and My Brother—A Case of Parricide in the 19th Century.* New York: Pantheon Books, 1975.

>Foucault and his students explore the time when crime became an object for medical discourse.

Foucault, Michel. *Discipline and Punish: The Birth of The Prison.* Alan Sheridan (tr.). New York: Vintage, 1979.
> Foucault examines the birth of the modern prison and the state of consciousness that it develops as a way to assure the automatic functioning of power.

Foucault, Michel. *Power/Knowledge: Selected Interviews and Other Writings.* Colin Gordon, ed. New York: Pantheon, 1980.
> This is a reasonably readable presentation of Foucault's main ideas.

Foucault, Michel, ed. *Herculine Barbin: Being the Recently Discovered Memoirs of a Nineteenth Century Hermaphrodite.* Brighton, England: Harvester Press, 1980.
> Foucault explores the tragic life of a person who grew up as a girl and then was later classified as a man. Through the presentation and analysis of the memoirs a powerful case is made about the way in which rigid sexual classification and control can obscure an individual's identity and lead to despair.

Fraser, Nancy. *Justice Interruptus: Critical Reflections on the Postsocialist Condition.* New York: Routledge, 1997.
> A feminist examination of the struggles for recognition of different identities and for the redistribution of material goods.

Freire, Paulo. *Pedagogy of the Oppressed.* London: Penguin, 1972.
> Freire describes his literacy program for a Third-World peasant community and develops a philosophy for educational emancipation of an underclass.

Geertz, Clifford. *The Interpretation of Cultures.* New York: Basic Books, 1973.
> Anthropologist Geertz argues that social science needs to develop rich descriptions of specific cultures, not universal generalizations.

Gilligan, Carol. *In a Different Voice: Psychological Theory and Woman's Development.* Cambridge, MA: Harvard University Press, 1982.
> Gilligan argues that moral theorists have been insensitive to the moral capacities of girls and have underemphasized the significance of an ethics of care.

Gutman, Amy. *Democratic Education.* Princeton, NJ: Princeton University Press, 1987.
> An analysis of the virtues and values of a democracy and the role of schooling in reproducing an open, free, and nonrepressive democratic society.

Gutman, Amy, ed. *Multiculturalism and the Politics of Recognition.* Princeton, NJ: Princeton University Press, 1994.
> Classic essays on the topic of multiculturalism with contributions by K. A. Taylor, Appiah, Habermas, and others.

Habermas, Jürgen. *Knowledge and Human Interest.* Boston: Beacon Press, 1968.
> Habermas attempts to reconcile an interpretivist view with traditional models of science by developing a critical theory of communication.

Haroutunian-Gordon, Sophie. *Turning the Soul.* Chicago: The University of Chicago Press, 1991.
> Provides a very informative description of the interpretive process as it develops in the teaching of *Romeo and Juliet* to a group of low-income, special education high school students.

Harré, Rom, and Secord, Paul. *The Explanation of Social Behaviour.* Totowa, NJ: Littlefield, Adams, 1973.
> Harré and Secord outline a new approach to social science that includes concern for human agency, rules, understandings, and interpretations.

Heath, Shirley Brice. *Ways with Words: Language, Life and Work in Communities and Classrooms.* Cambridge, England: Cambridge University Press, 1983.
> Uses interpretivist methods to explore the ways in which children from different cultures learn to use language and shows the contrast between language learning at home and at school.

hooks, bell. *Teaching to Transgress.* Boston: Beacon Press, 1991.
> A classic text on schooling, race, and critical theory.

Karabel, Jerome, and Halsey, A. H., eds. *Power and Ideology in Education.* New York: Oxford University Press, 1977.
> Presents some of the major positions in the sociology of education and provides different ways to view the relationship between schooling and power.

Krausz, Michael, and Meiland, Jack W., eds. *Relativism: Cognitive and Moral.* Notre Dame, IN: University of Notre Dame Press, 1982.
> Explores the meaning and implications of relativism in both the cognitive and moral domains and provides a critical appraisal of the relativist point of view.

Kuhn, Thomas S. *The Structure of Scientific Revolutions.* Chicago: The University of Chicago Press, 1962; 2nd enl. ed., 1970.
> This classic essay in the history of science challenges traditional views of science and raises important issues about the possibility of objective knowledge.

Lemann, Nicholas. *The Big Test: The Secret History of the American Meritocracy.* New York: Farrar, Strauss, and Giroux, 2000.
> A history of the development of the testing movement.

Lightfoot, Sara Lawrence. *The Good High School.* New York: Basic Books, 1983.
> An interpretivist study of five very different secondary schools.

MacIntyre, Alasdair. *Whose Justice? Which Rationality?* Notre Dame, IN: University of Notre Dame Press, 1988.
> Explores the complexities involved in multiple interpretations and seeks to develop a way of choosing between different interpretations.

MacKinnon, Catharine. *Feminism Unmodified: Discourses on Life and Law.* Cambridge, MA: Harvard University Press, 1987.
> Explores reasons why women have not benefited from equal rights legislation.

Meier, Deborah. *In Schools We Trust: Creating Communities of Learning in an Era of Testing and Standardization.* Boston: Beacon Press, 2002.
> A passionate analysis of the social forces at work in the turn to high-stakes testing, including a discussion of the No Child Left Behind Act.

Noddings, Nel. *Caring: A Feminist Approach to Ethics & Moral Education.* Berkeley: University of California Press, 1984.
> A feminist's account of the ethics of care and its application to the teacher–student relationship.

Parsons, Talcott. *The Social System.* Glencoe, IL: Free Press, 1951.
> Parsons develops his classic framework for a functionalist sociology.

Peshkin, Alan. *The Color of Strangers, the Color of Friends.* Chicago: The University of Chicago Press, 1991.
> Uses interpretivist methods to explore the interactions among different groups in a large, multiethnic high school.

Phillips, D. C. *Philosophy, Science and Social Inquiry.* Oxford, England: Pergamon Press, 1987.
> An excellent set of essays clarifying basic issues in the debates between positivist and interpretivist researchers.

Popkewitz, Thomas, and Fendler, Lynn, eds. *Critical Theories in Education: Changing Terrains of Knowledge and Politics.* New York: Routledge, 1999.
> Essays on the state of critical theory in education.

Reich, Robert. *The Future of Success.* New York: Knopf, 2001.
> A social analysis of the world high school and college graduates enter.

Rorty, Richard. *Philosophy and Social Hope.* Cambridge, England: Cambridge University Press, 2000.
> An introduction to Rorty's contributions to modern American social thought.

Sleeter, Christine E., ed. *Empowerment Through Multi-Cultural Education.* Albany: State University of New York Press, 1990.
> Ethnographic studies examining the disempowerment of children from oppressed groups and the potential of empowerment through multicultural education.

Strike, Kenneth. *Liberal Justice and the Marxist Critique: A Study of Conflicting Research Programs.* New York: Routledge, 1989.
> Compares functionalist/liberal theories of society and schooling with Marxist views. Strike finds much of the Marxist critique to be on target, but he ultimately defends a liberal democratic conception of justice and educating.

Weis, Lois. *Working Class Without Work: High School Students in De-Industrializing America.* New York: Routledge, 1990.
> An interpretivist study that explores how young people in school struggle with their own identity formation as members of a working-class family in a radically changing society that is different from that of their parents.

Westheimer, Joel. *Among School Teachers: Community, Autonomy, and Ideology in Teachers' Work.* New York: Teachers College Press, 1998.
> A trenchant analysis of the work that teachers do, with attention to the ideological and social forces at play in schools.

Winch, Peter. *The Idea of Social Science and Its Relation to Philosophy.* London: Routledge and Kegan Paul, 1958.
> A philosophical argument for viewing social science as an interpretive study

Young, Michael F. D., ed. *Knowledge and Control: New Directions for the Sociology of Education.* London: Collier-Macmillan, 1971.
> The contributors to this volume challenge the dominant mode of functionalist and positivist research and apply an interpretivist perspective to the study of schooling.